TAKUNDA AARON CHIMUTASHU

Becoming King

Becoming a True Leader , As Seen From A Black Boy's Eyes

This books is based on true the life events of the author and is inspired by, and in most instances draws upon, factual events. However, it should be noted that the character names, dialogue, and specific incidents depicted within are fictionalized and do not purport to portray any real individual or event with verifiable accuracy.

First edition

This book was professionally typeset on Reedsy.
Find out more at reedsy.com

Contents

Foreword

Writing this book was a deeply emotional experience that required me to dig deep into memories of my childhood. This process was made easier by the continued emotional support of my loving partner and her willingness over the years to listen to constant retellings of these stories and the impact they have had on me as a person. To be able to share such a core memory is a massive honor and I thank you, dear reader, for picking this book up and giving it a whirl.

Preface

This book isn't a sanitized guide to climbing the corporate, political or social ladders; it's a candid exploration of leadership in all its aspects, forged in the crucible of a marginalized community. It's a fire guard designed to channel the ambition that burns within you, inspiring you to stand up and do right by those who follow your lead.

As a child, responsibility wasn't a choice, it was a weight I bore alongside my friends, many mirroring my experience of single-parent homes and loss. Where others saw childhood games, we saw battlegrounds where wars were fought for our only sanctuary - the playground. We weren't just playing; we were strategizing, forming alliances, and navigating the complex social hierarchy with the raw instinct and fierce ambition of youth.

These weren't mere playground squabbles; they were lessons in leadership learned in the most unexpected classroom. Fueled by movies where heroes faced life-or-death choices, our small community became an incubator for untamed leadership. This book captures that journey, not through the lens of an expert, but as a fellow traveler sharing hard-won lessons.

Forget the lofty pronouncements of leadership gurus. Here,

you'll encounter the unfiltered reality of a childhood where every move held serious stakes. Prepare to see leadership through fresh, unfiltered eyes, where playground alliances and childhood rivalries hold potent truths about power, influence, and the responsibility that comes with both.

Join me on this exploration of leadership redefined. Not through philosophical theories, but through the gritty reality of a marginalized community where leadership wasn't about climbing the ladder, but using it to pull others up.

I

To see through the eyes of a child is a privilege beyond privilege. Approaching all things with curious innocence, children have the unique ability to see things as they are or as they could be, never dwelling on preconceived notion...never seeing them as they were
-Me, A Grown African Man

1

Rebelling Against Injustice

My earliest memory of witnessing an injustice comes from a time when I was no more than 9 years old. My family was living at a massive flat complex called Eastview Gardens which had at least 700 flats divided into 7 courts, each named after Zimbabwean rivers. My family lived at the biggest court, Odzi, and as such my friend group, comprising of Jacob, Tadiwa, Paida (Tadiwa's little brother), and myself, was exclusive to Odzi.

Our friend group, though tiny, had a clear hierarchy. Jacob was our leader partially because he was the fastest among us (and speed was a massive status symbol at this age), but mostly because his family was well of enough to afford a DSTV (cable) subscription and we needed to keep him happy if we were going to get invited to watch cartoons and anime at his house. Jacob was more than aware of this and would often punish us for disobeying or defying him by refusing us access to precious entertainment.

I was the second in command because I had an old Phillips game station that I had inherited from my older brother and used as leverage to stay in good books with Jacob. Tadiwa and Paida's parents on the other hand had invested heavily into toys for their kids and toys, though common, were still a valuable resource. We knew that just including Tadiwa, our age mate, would be enough to secure the toys, but Paida was like a little brother to us and I held a soft spot in my heart for the kid so he was always invited to hang out.

One fine day, my pals and I were seated in a small circle discussing the last episode of Dragon Ball Z and we were paying keen attention to our leader, Jacob, as he described what he believed would most likely happen in the next episode. You couldn't interrupt Jacob when he was mid speech, or you would risk missing episodes of the exclusive shows. This was a well established, though silently enforced, rule so you can imagine our surprise when little Paida suddenly piped up with an opinion of his own.

"Nah, you're wrong."

None of us had actually been listening to Jacob, but this sudden incursion into his awful monologue cut through our boredom like a scalpel. What was Paida thinking? He might never get to find out what happens in the episode. Granted the boy was only 6, but he knew better. As I was processing this novel event, Jacob stood up quietly and, with no hesitation whatsoever, kicked Paida in the belly so hard, he slid backward a little.

What happened next was one of the most shameful memories I

have to this day. Tadiwa, Paida's brother, and I froze. We looked at Paida, writhing on the ground and struggling to breath, then at Jacob, standing over him with an evil smile on his face and finally at each other. In this moment we quietly weighed our options. Jacob wasn't a large boy and with our forces combined, we could definitely take him. This path would doubtless lead to us being cut off from DSTV and all the wonderful shows on it and possibly destroy our friend group for ever. On the other hand, we could do nothing, sit back, let Paida recover and laugh about it some other day between marathon episodes of Dragon Ball Z.

We chose the latter.

I stood up and started trying to convince Jacob to let it go while Tadiwa managed to get Paida to his feet and lead him home. What we didn't know in that moment was that Jacob had done some serious damage and little Paida would need surgery to repair some internal injuries. It would be months before the kid was the same physically, but mentally he was changed for ever. I wish I had stood up for my little buddy. It wouldn't have spared him the surgeries, but at the very least, he would have known he has someone looking out for him. Instead, I chose personal benefit over my friend and I will never forgive myself for that.

The Price of Silence

The world, like our childhood playground in Odzi Court, is filled with power imbalances. There are vast and mighty empires that, like Jacob, command resources and wield influence with an iron fist. Then there are nations, smaller and often poorer, navigating the intricacies of this power play like we tiptoed around Jacob's fragile ego. And the question that forever echoes, the shadow always lurking - are we complicit in the injustices we witness, the Paidas left battered and broken, because of the crumbs of comfort tossed from the imperial table?

History whispers this tale in countless tones. Rome, the colossus that cast its long shadow across the ancient world, demanded fealty from smaller kingdoms. Trade agreements, yes, but often laced with the bitter aftertaste of tribute and of subservience. Kingdoms like Numidia, once fiercely independent, found themselves caught in the dance of diplomacy and desperation, a waltz between economic dependence and the threat of military might. Did those kingdoms truly hold autonomy, or did they, like us frozen in Odzi Court, become silent bystanders to atrocities committed against their neighbors, all for the sake of maintaining ties with the empire?

The modern stage reflects a similar drama, though played out in boardrooms and diplomatic cables instead. The United States, the undisputed superpower of our time, casts a long shadow across the globe, its influence stretching from trade deals to military interventions. And just as smaller nations sought Rome's favor, many today wrestle with the ethical tightrope of engaging with the Eagle. Economic opportunities dangle like Jacob's tantalizing DSTV subscription, promising development and prosperity. But the price, sometimes, is silence in the face of the powerful nation's transgressions.

Take the case of Angola, a nation rich in oil and strategic advantage. In the 1980s, amidst a brutal civil war, the US, seeking to counter Soviet influence, forged close ties with Angola's UNITA rebel group, led by Jonas Savimbi. The US provided military and financial aid, turning a blind eye to Savimbi's human rights abuses, including the use of child soldiers and the displacement of millions. While the US's support ultimately helped end the war, it came at a heavy cost – an estimated 500,000 lives lost and a legacy of instability that continues to plague Angola today.

The Angolan story is not an isolated one. Nations rich in oil and strategic advantage find themselves entangled in a complex web of alliances with the US, their economies buoyed by military contracts and trade partnerships. Yet, when human rights violations occur under those alliances, when drone strikes cast their deadly shadows, does the silence of allies and benefactors not become complicity? Do we, like Tadiwa and I, turn our backs on the Paidas of those distant lands, sacrificing their cries for justice for the sake of our own economic well-being and safety?This silence is not without its consequences. It emboldens the powerful, fuels injustice, and ultimately undermines the very values of freedom and democracy that these nations claim to uphold.

But just as there are those who remain silent, there are also whispers of courage, echoes of defiance that refuse to be drowned out by the excuse of economic pragmatism. These whispers come from individuals and groups who dare to speak truth to power, who stand shoulder-to-shoulder with the Paidas of the world, demanding justice and accountability.

One such voice is Angolan journalist Rafael Marques, who for years has risked his life to expose the human rights abuses committed by both the Angolan government and its allies. Marques's investigations have led to international condemnation, sanctions, and even the arrest of high-ranking officials. He is a testament to the power of a single voice, a reminder that even in the face of overwhelming odds, courage and conviction can make a difference.

This is not to paint with the simplistic brush of good versus evil. The world is rarely so binary. Engagement with powerful nations can indeed bring development, foster peace, and offer a path to progress. But that engagement must be tempered with a clear moral compass, a refusal to compromise core values for temporary gain. Just as we, in our moment of cowardice, should have confronted Jacob's cruelty, nations must not shy away from speaking truth to power.

Condemning human rights abuses, pushing for accountability, standing shoulder-to-shoulder with the Paidas of the world - these are not acts of hostility, but of moral clarity. They are the echoes of defiance that refuse to be drowned out by the siren song of economic benefit. They are the whispers of courage that remind us that true sovereignty lies not in silent servitude, but in the unwavering pursuit of justice for all.

The choice, like that faced in Odzi Court, is never easy. The risks are real, the potential consequences dire. But as we navigate the intricate politics of this global playground, let us remember: the silence of bystanders, the turning away from injustice, ultimately becomes a chorus of condoning. To truly stand tall, to be a person worthy of respect, you must not only demand justice for yourself, but for the Paidas of the world, even when their pain echoes from lands far beyond the shadow of our own court.

Seizing Power

Jacob had to go.

Tadiwa and I never explicitly discussed Jacob's demise, but we were markedly aware of each other's rage. The first step would be to replace the most precious thing he offered, entertainment. Initially we begged our respective parents to install DSTV. Though we could not clearly articulate why we needed it, we became an incessant nagging presence to our parents. Days passed and no progress was made, instead they would bribe us with useless (but truly appreciated) gifts of candy and extra pocket money.

One day, having both received this extra money, Tadiwa and I left Paida (who was still healing from his injury) and headed to a small market by the complex gate behind Odzi court. We took a short cut, but Odzi was so massive it took us ages to go from one end to the other. The day was hot but Odzi, the 5 floor, 200 apartment sprawling behemoth it was, cast a massive shadow that kept us in the cool shade the whole way. We got our ice cold freezits (frozen flavored drinks in thin plastic bags) and as we sucked on our prize, we chose to take the long way back. This time, we had our eyes opened. There were so many kids.

As I mentioned earlier, Odzi had 200 apartments. Lets assume for a moment that only half of those had families with one kid. That's 100 kids. Lets push it further and assume only half of those kids were in our age group. That's an estimated 50 kids! A small number objectively, but massive compared to our tiny 4 person friend group. Jacob had occasionally accepted outsiders joining us to play games and the like, but not once had the sheer number of potential resource holders struck us.

One of these kids had DSTV. And we were about to find and befriend the hell out of them.

Our efforts weren't very coordinated, but eventually, we had expanded our friend ground considerably and formed a superhero team of sorts. Jacob was the fastest, so we needed a fast kid and that's where Simba came in. A primary school athlete and one of the fastest kids we had ever met, Simba was a lot faster than Jacob. Next, DSTV. For that we had Dereck and Aaron. Keep in mind my name was Aaron too so we needed to differentiate new Aaron from me. In true Kids Next Door fashion, we decided he would be Number 2 and I would be called Number 1 or simply Aaron 1. Plus, as an added advantage, Number 2 was a big kid, standing a full head taller than all of us.

It wasn't long before Jacob was entirely irrelevant. We didn't tolerate his outbursts anymore and any physical nonsense was often quickly contained by Number 2. At some point my mother's defenses finally fell and she got us a limited DSTV subscription and suddenly I was among the elite. Gradually, we stopped listening to or hanging out with Jacob entirely and started doing what we wanted to do on our terms. It had taken nearly a month, but we had finally secured our freedom.

By the time Paida returned, we came back to a hero's welcome. He was embraced by strangers who would soon become his closest and most faithful friends. A little while later, we heard a rumor that Jacob's family had moved out of Eastview Gardens. We quickly ran to the top floor to investigate and, finding their apartment empty, stood stunned. We had felled the beast (obviously we had nothing to do with them moving, but him being gone felt nice all the same). But now there was a power vacuum. Or so I thought.

From Shadows to Sovereignty

The tale of Jacob's demise in Odzi Court whispers a timeless truth about the rise and fall of empires throughout history and presents valuable lessons for our entrepreneurial journey. Just as Tadiwa and I united our ragtag band to overthrow the tyranny held up by DSTV access, so too can you, with strategic alliances and unwavering courage, carve your own path in the daunting world of business.

Think of the Ashanti Confederacy, a formidable alliance of Akan kingdoms in West Africa who resisted European encroachment for over a century. They forged trade pacts, pooled military resources, and adopted innovative warfare tactics, culminating in the Battle of Nsamankow (1888), a resounding victory that threatened British colonial ambitions. Though ultimately subdued, the Ashanti's spirit of unity and resilience echoed through the continent.

Across the Atlantic, the Haitian Revolution stands as a testament to the power of collective action. Enslaved Africans from diverse ethnicities and backgrounds joined forces, forging alliances across linguistic barriers to overthrow French colonial rule. The Haitian victory in 1804 sent shockwaves through the Americas, proving that even the mightiest empires could be toppled by the united will of the oppressed.

The tale of our playground rebellion against Jacob's tyranny echoes in the boardrooms of powerful corporations as well. Just like we, as ragtag kids, challenged the established rule, several airlines in the 1970s dared to stand up to the mighty Pan Am, the undisputed king of transatlantic travel. Pan Am, wielding its monopolistic power, dictated routes, prices, and alliances, squeezing profits from passengers and airlines alike. But whispers of defiance soon turned into a collective roar.

In 1979, a group of airlines, including TWA, British Airways, Lufthansa, and KLM, formed the "International Association of Machinists and Aerospace Workers" (IAMAW). This unlikely alliance, much like our ragtag group in Odzi Court, was a diverse bunch with varying interests. Yet, they were united by a common enemy: Pan Am's dominance.

The IAMAW employed various tactics to chip away at Pan Am's control. They negotiated lower fuel prices for their members, challenged Pan Am's control over key routes, and even launched aggressive marketing campaigns highlighting Pan Am's high fares and restrictive policies.

The impact was undeniable. Pan Am's market share steadily declined, forcing them to lower fares and loosen their grip on routes. More importantly, the IAMAW paved the way for deregulation in the airline industry, opening up competition and ultimately leading to the downfall of Pan Am's monopoly. This victory, much like our playground triumph, wasn't just about toppling a tyrant, but about creating a level playing field where everyone could benefit.

Across continents, another coalition reflects our defiance, this time in the realm of Tech. The Open Handset Alliance (OHA), formed in 2007, is a diverse consortium of tech giants like Google, Samsung, and LG. In the face of the dominant closed-source operating system of the time, they joined forces to develop the Android platform, an open-source alternative that empowers users and fosters innovation. Their story, like our rebellion against the limited access to Jacob's DSTV, is a testament to the power of collaboration in breaking down technological monopolies and democratizing access for millions.

These contemporary triumphs, like the echoes of the Ashanti and Haitian revolutions, offer invaluable lessons for navigating the global power dynamics of today. Whether facing economic giants, digital behemoths, or any form of oppressive rule, collective action remains the weapon of choice for the powerless. Trade agreements, regional alliances, and open-source initiatives are the slingshots and cunning strategies that can topple the titans of our time.

These stories, like countless others etched in the annals of history, offer lessons for the contemporary world. In the face of economic disparity and political oppression, nations can find strength in unity. Trade pacts, like the African Continental Free Trade Area, can foster economic independence, while regional alliances, like the African Union, can provide a platform for collective action against external threats.

Yet, the path to freedom is rarely smooth. Internal rivalries, resource constraints, and external manipulation can threaten to fracture alliances, just as finding the new leader of our little friend group posed a challenge to our new found unity. However, by upholding the principles of shared prosperity, strategic cooperation, and unwavering commitment to justice, even the most unlikely coalitions can emerge from the shadows of empires and claim their rightful place on the world stage.

The struggle for freedom, whether played out on the lush lawns of Odzi Court or the boardrooms of global corporations, is ultimately a story of collective courage, strategic collaboration, and the unwavering pursuit of justice. It is a reminder that even the smallest voice, raised in unison with others, can become a chorus that resonates with power, eventually toppling the mightiest empires and paving the way for a future where equity and opportunity flow freely for all.

West Africa and Haiti may have found independence, but the quest for economic and political stability still continues. PAn Am may have loosened its grip, but the fight for fair trade continues. The open-source revolution may have democratized technology, but the battle for digital rights rages on. And just like the group and I stood tall against Jacob's tyranny, millions across the globe fight against various forms of oppression, their collective voices echoing the timeless truth whispered by the tale of Odzi Court – that no empire, no matter how mighty, can withstand the relentless tide of united defiance

A New Day

One of Jacob's favorite games was called "open gates". Basically we would find a bunch of kids and divide ourselves into two groups. One group would stand on the far side of a field and the other would stand in the middle. group one's mission was to get to the other side of the field one at a time, whilst group 2's mission was to catch as many daring aspirants from group 2 as possible and by so doing, recruit them to their own team. If any one member of group 1 made it to the other side, they would declare "open gates!" allowing the entirety of group 1 to rush to the other side, often confusing and dividing the efforts of group 2. It was a fun game that had the potential to make us many friends, but Jacob had always ruined it with his egotistical rants and constant refusal to accept defeat or victory with grace.

Now, in this moment, this glorious moment of true freedom, we could do what we wanted, how we wanted. I turned to my friends and saw them all looking at me. Or rather, looking *to me,* as if to say "now what?".

I had been second in command for ages and not once had it crossed my mind what would happen if our first in command was deposed. I was the leader now. My rule would determine the future of our little group. I would be fair. I would undo the awfulness that Jacob wrought and usher in a period of joy for my friends. I would do this leadership thing right. I smiled and said, with both authority and elation,

"Lets play open gates."

2

Claiming The Mantle

Our friend group had grown from a 4 to 6 and we were happier than ever. We had a surplus of everything and even when some of us went on vacation with our families, there were always enough redundancies where DSTV and toys were concerned. My primary issue was that of speed and I practiced daily (even at school) until I found myself capable of beating everyone but Simba. My leadership though, was often challenged. It didn't happen randomly, it was almost always during highly physical games like play fighting.

We used to watch a lot of WWE (World Wrestling Entertainment) back then, enamored by the stunts and fights, and despite the show constantly imploring us "Do not try this at home or at school," we tried it. Just like WWE, our rules were simple, if you could get your opponent to quit the match or pin them for 3 seconds, you win. It was during this "trying" that someone large like Number 2 or someone especially agile like Tadiwa would attempt to best me. If any one of us won enough times they basically earned the right to switch the game to whatever they wanted to play, thereby assuming temporary leadership of the gang. A massive threat indeed. But in this threat, I saw an opportunity.

Within the WWE, there were characters who were known for their incredible tank like physique. Characters that required coordinated teamwork for other wrestlers to beat them. These tanks would sometimes be used to sell the audience a new character who, during their introduction, would defeat the tank and solidify themselves as a really good wrestler and a genuine threat in just one match. This was often a feel good moment for both the newly introduced character and for the audience, who got to witness an underdog victory. The tank would later have his reputation restored by performing an insane feat of strength or invincibility, like getting hit by a chair and not flinching, and the whole cycle would start over. Some of the greatest wrestlers of all time got boosts from tanks. Moreover, tanks often gave us the opportunity to witness our favorite wrestlers team up in order to defeat them. These tanks were star makers and true legends.

One of Jacob's greatest weaknesses had been his inability to lose with grace. Paired with his constant bossy demeanor and refusal to take suggestions, this had made him an obnoxious little dictator. I would not fall to such practices. Instead, as I trained myself to be fast, I needed to train myself to be a tank. I needed to learn to take a hit. To achieve my goal I would stay behind at school and challenge fellow wrestling enthusiasts to take me down, make me tap or make sure I couldn't get up. Initially it was pretty easy for them to best me, but eventually I became sturdier and a lot harder to hurt, pin or defeat in any way. The plan was coming together.

One day as my Odzi friends and I were play fighting, I got hit by Tadiwa and didn't budge. He pushed me and I pushed him off of me with enough force to send him reeling. This caught the attention of the rest of the gang and very quickly they teamed up and started coordinating their strikes. I didn't make it easy, but eventually they took me down.

Next, I took tiny little Paida on in a one on one match. I made it especially hard on him. I made sure not to agitate his now healed wound and I definitely took more hits than I gave out, but the little guy, now exhausted, was getting desperate. So, in true WWE fashion, Paida rallied the crowd. He raise his tiny hands over his head and yelled at the top of his lungs. Our small gang cheered him on. He was facing a monster they had fought hard to best as a team after all. With his final burst of strength, Paida jumped on me, forced me to my knees and performed a stunt known as a "DDT" wherein he slams my head into the ground. It did not hurt one bit, and yet, I stayed down. Paida leaped onto me and pinned me. Number 2 instantly morphed into a referee, slid across the "ring" and gave the three count.

1, 2, 3. Paida wins, and the crowd goes wild.

I stood up slowly, overselling my injuries, and joined my gang in congratulating the underdog. Number 2 patted my back and gave me a knowing smile. He knew exactly what had happened and respected me all the more for it. They all did.

In that moment, our play fighting had transformed from a

struggle for power to an opportunity for all of us to display humility and have fun. Paida, being so fabulously victorious, picked the next game and we tried a game we had never heard of or played before (something involving fairy godmothers and wishes). This became our way of life. We learned from each other, learned to respect each other and everyone became so happy and satisfied that my leadership was never challenged again.

Lessons in Leadership and Learning

My childish efforts to find ways to defy the old tradition and evolve myself into a leader better suited for my group hold a profound truth about leadership, not just for my friends and I, but for the countless figures throughout history who have shaped the destinies of nations and organisations. Here we find an allegory for the kind of leaders we often yearn for – those who prioritize not dominance, but growth, not their own egos, but the collective well-being of their people.

Across continents and centuries, we find compelling illustrations of this principle. Consider Mansa Musa, the 14th-century emperor of Mali. Renowned for his immense wealth and extravagance, Musa was also a fervent patron of learning. He established universities in Timbuktu, transforming the city into a hub of intellectual exchange. His reign saw a flourishing of literature, astronomy, and architecture, a testament to his understanding that true power lies not just in gold, but in fostering a culture of knowledge and growth.

Across the continent, in the bustling kingdom of 16th century Benin, flourished Queen Idia, a figure of wisdom and resilience. Though never officially the monarch, her influence on her son, Ewuare the Great, proved monumental. Ewuare, was a young leader faced with the challenge of uniting a fractured kingdom. Heeding his mother's counsel, Ewuare embraced diplomacy and cultural assimilation, establishing guilds, promoting trade, and fostering artistic expression. Under his reign, Benin became a beacon of peace, prosperity, and artistic innovation.

In Tanzania, Julius Nyerere embodied the spirit of humility and collaborative leadership. A staunch advocate for pan-Africanism and socialist ideals, Nyerere prioritized education and rural development. He encouraged collective decision-making and empowered local communities, recognizing that true progress rests not on top-down dictates, but on the participation and growth of all citizens.

These lessons echo in the boardrooms of global corporations and the halls of government too. Consider Anita Roddick, the founder of The Body Shop. In the 1960s, Roddick defied the cosmetics industry with a radical vision – sustainable beauty products, fair trade practices, and ethical activism. She embraced vulnerability, publicly criticizing animal testing and environmental abuse, even as corporate giants mocked her small business. But through relentless learning and adaptation, Roddick grew The Body Shop into a global brand, proving that authentic leadership can flourish beyond traditional power structures.

Across the Atlantic, Yvon Chouinard, the founder of Patagonia, another unconventional leader, offers a different perspective. Recognizing the limitations of traditional capitalism, Chouinard, in 2018, transferred ownership of Patagonia, valued at over $3 billion, to a trust dedicated to fighting climate change. This revolutionary act, like Paida's unexpected victory, challenged assumptions about corporate purpose and redefined the role of businesses in society. Chouinard's leadership embodies the idea that true power lies not in hoarding wealth, but in leveraging resources for a greater good.

Closer to home, Wangari Maathai, the Nobel Peace Prize-winning Kenyan environmentalist, serves as a beacon of collective empowerment. Faced with deforestation and widespread poverty, Maathai, like Queen Idia guiding Ewuare, didn't impose solutions. Instead, she founded the Green Belt Movement, mobilizing rural women to plant trees and restore their communities. By nurturing local leadership and fostering collective action, Maathai's legacy reminds us that sustainable progress happens when everyone holds the power to grow.

But the path of enlightened leadership is rarely without its pitfalls. Historical figures encountered resistance from those threatened by their commitment to learning and collective advancement. Mansa Musa's attempts to reform the gold trade generated resentment from established merchants, while Queen Idia had to raise armies to solidify her son's rule. Even Nyerere, despite his popularity, faced internal dissent and economic challenges in his quest to create a more equitable Tanzania. In the world of business, Roddick faced lawsuits from competitors and criticism from those threatened by her ethical stances, Chouinard's decision to give away Patagonia sparked controversy and legal challenges and Maathai faced political intimidation and resistance from vested interests.

This inherent tension between the desire for learning and growth and the resistance of those clinging to old power structures underscores the crucial role of humility in genuine leadership. Just as I embraced vulnerability and allowed Paida to "pin" me, so too must leaders possess the humility to learn from their people, acknowledge their own limitations, and create spaces for open dialogue and diverse perspectives.

This doesn't imply relinquishing responsibility, but rather shifting the focus from ego to shared purpose and open dialogue.

The true mark of a leader isn't the brute force of a dictator, but the wisdom of a mentor, the humility of a learner, and the unwavering commitment to building a just and equitable society where everyone, like my friends and I, can find their place and celebrate the joy of shared victory.

This is not a call for passive acceptance, but for cultivating a culture of critical thinking, constructive debate, and mutual respect – one where the Paidas of the world can not only rise above their immediate struggles, but can also contribute their unique perspectives and talents to the larger tapestry of the nation. This is the challenge, and the promise, of enlightened leadership in the 21st century.

The echoes of "open gates" and "DDTs" may seem trivial on the surface, but they offer a powerful reminder: true leadership often lies not in imposing one's vision, but in creating an environment where all voices can be heard, all minds can grow, and all citizens can contribute to a brighter future.

The Power and Dangers of Belief

If you are starting to think this book is all about how perfect I was and how everyone needs to be like me, then that perspective is about to take a massive turn.

It was a week day and we were preparing to play some after school open gates, but for some reason Tadiwa was nowhere to be seen. I couldn't start a game this important without my best friend, so I started quizzing everyone about his whereabouts. Paida had shown up so I directed my inquiries about his brother to him.

"He got hurt at school. He doesn't feel like playing".

I had once watched Tadiwa get tackled in a game of open gates, land hard on the ground and get up a minute later, so the idea that he was so badly hurt he couldn't play was worrying. We ended the game and went to check on my second in command. We got to their apartment and waited outside respectfully whilst Paida went in to fetch his brother. Paida returned alone and beckoned me to enter. I signaled the gang to stay outside and I went in alone. I had never really been inside Tadiwa and Paida's house. Their parents insisted we play with their toys outside and none of us had ever dared defy them. Not to mention Paida's injury had not really shined a positive light on us since we had refused to snitch on Jacob, despite his overt cruelty.

Tadiwa was seated on the couch watching TV. He looked perfectly fine and calmly acknowledged my presence. The afternoon shows on TV were pretty good, but the best ones started an hour from now so he obviously was not blowing us off for cartoons.

"Some kids at school bullied me. I don't feel like playing right now"

I looked to the floor, silent. Tadiwa's school was so far away his parents had to drop him off with their car. I knew I could probably confront these bullies, but how exactly would I get there? I was useless to him. Looking back, Tadiwa probably needed a comforting hand and some kindness, but my prepubescent brain was all hopped up on Dragon Ball Z and Kung fu movies. I could have said anything. Literally anything else, instead I said,

"I know a deadly fighting style. I went to China when I was a kid and I learned to fight there. I can teach you if you want."

Beyond the stunt filled wrestling of the WWE, I had never actually learned to fight. I had just lied to my best friend. He lit up and begged me to teach him everything I knew. I feigned hesitation and then channeled every martial arts master I had seen from the movies.

"I will teach you."

What I didn't predict was that Tadiwa would not only be the most devoted trainee, but that he would tell the rest of the group. Suddenly, everyone wanted to learn the "deadly fighting style". My lie was getting out of hand and I needed a solution. First, I knew that every martial arts movie depicted loads of calisthenics, strength training, endurance training, and flexibility training. I would start there. For weeks, the boys and I did push ups, sit ups, pull ups and ran the entire 1-1.5km course of the circular road connecting the whole of Eastview Gardens. Non-stop, we trained and grew stronger. Eventually, we extended our running track to cover the outside of the Eastview Gardens perimeter. We got tough. Real tough.

The whole time we were doing this training, I was consuming and practicing as much martial arts lore as I could. I joined Karate class, started a proper amateur wrestling club at school (the one they do at the Olympics, not our WWE stuff) and watched even more martial arts movies than usual. I learned how to punch and kick properly and started practicing punching walls and taking strikes to my abs. If I was going to train bad asses, I needed to be a bad ass. I had lied my way into learning to fight and learn to fight I would.

By the time I was ready to start slowly imparting knowledge on my eager students, I had developed a style of my own that was a weird amalgamation of movie nonsense and real world martial arts. They ate it up. Based on my lie I had gone from an unofficial leader to "Sensei" and the power I wielded now extended far beyond choosing games. I could, at any point, declare push up time, a random test of strength or demand we all get into formation and practice our punches till dusk. To keep everyone motivated, I would often embellish on my lies and claim to have won fictitious tournaments and met masters far greater than myself who imparted me with great wisdom and power. My friends submitted all their free time to learning everything I could teach.

It was intoxicating.

Lies, Power, and the Peril of Deification

My lie about a "deadly fighting style" transcends a mere playground fib; it illuminates the dangerous dance between leadership, blind faith, and the dangers of deifying human figures. Tales like this are fairly common within the grand opera of global history, offering cautionary echoes from leaders across Africa and beyond who wielded deception as a tool of governance, both for noble and nefarious ends.

On the noble end, think of the many war time revolutionary leaders who brought an end to colonial rule. Some are recorded as having used carefully crafted narratives of anti-colonial victory, the glories of war and broad national unity to rally people behind their visions and recruit new soldiers. These narratives, while containing elements of truth, often glossed over internal dissent and the gruesome realities of war. To inspire their people, who were fighting for freedom and true liberation from oppression, these leaders needed to blend charisma and calculated deception and this proved effective in mobilizing support for their causes, albeit at the cost of suppressing dissent and sometimes fostering a personality cult.

In Uganda, Idi Amin presented a stark contrast. His was no noble cause. His was an endeavor of pure ego and lust for power. His rise to power was built on a web of fabrications, portraying himself as a champion of the marginalized while purging political opponents and orchestrating brutal ethnic cleansing. Amin's reign, riddled with outlandish claims and outright lies, was a chilling example of how deception can be used to consolidate power and crush any semblance of accountability.

The dangers of unchecked power and blind faith are ever-present. My lie, initially a desperate attempt to assist a friend in peril, snowballed into a web of fabricated tales and escalating demands. My friends, blinded by admiration and eager to learn the mythical "deadly fighting style," surrendered their time and trust, placing me on a pedestal far above my human limitations. This dynamic echoes throughout history, from the deification of ancient pharaohs to the contemporary cult-like followings of some political leaders today!

The consequences of such deification are often dire. Leaders wielding the power granted by unquestioning faith become increasingly unaccountable, their lies and excesses masked by the aura of infallibility. Dissent is stifled, criticism silenced, and entire societies can find themselves trapped in a cage of recklessly manufactured reality.

The lesson here, then, is a nuanced one. Deception in the hands of a leader, whether used for righteous or dubious purposes, can be a double-edged sword. While it may offer short-term benefits, the long-term cost of fostering blind faith and unchecked power is often far greater.

True leadership isn't about a web of lies and manufactured personas. It relies in humility, transparency, and the courage to face challenges as equals, not gods. Leaders, no matter how charismatic or skilled, are but human, fallible creatures. Embracing this, fostering open dialogue and robust debate, is the antidote to the poison of unquestioning faith and the deification of leaders.

Only by rejecting the lies and recognizing the pitfalls of blind faith can we build societies where leaders are held accountable, where truth, not deception, forms the bedrock of governance, and where power is shared, contested, and never allowed to rest solely on the shoulders of a self-proclaimed "Sensei."

Beyond Belief.

In time, Tadiwa successfully fought off his bullies. Even little Paida started receiving respect from kids throughout Odzi court who bore witness to our consistent training exercises. The myth was starting to extend far beyond me and shrouding my gang. No longer were we the "Open Gates Organizers," we were the fighters. No bully, at Odzi or at school, dared challenge us. We remained dedicated to our training and I even expanded elements of it to include even more martial arts I was beginning to diligently (and earnestly) study.

It was awful of me to start and maintain such a beautiful journey from such a deceptive stand point, but I just gotten started.

You see, my limitations were quite clear. As much as I was a sensei, I was still a kid, subject to the disciplinary measures of adults. Parents, teachers, guards (tasked with maintaining order at Eastview Gardens) and even strange adults all presented a massive threat to my control and power. I needed something beyond simple belief and trust.

I needed to create *faith*.

3

Faith, Power & Darkness

Besides Dragon Ball Z, we had a short list of anime that we truly enjoyed and bonded over. The best of these was "Beyblade". The anime revolved around a group of kids who grew to be friends. They used to battle each other through highly advanced spinning tops called Beyblades that would clash in an arena and demolish each other until only one was left spinning and the other could spin no more. It was a fairly simple concept, but it wouldn't be anime if it did not go a step further.

Each person who had a beyblade also had a "Bit Beast". I'm not quite sure if they were spiritual or technological (its fairly vague), but a Bit Beast was a totem creature that possessed and empowered your beyblade. The more powerful your bit beast, the more powerful your beyblade. Sure you could upgrade the actual beyblade itself, but it was the relationship between beyblader and bit beast that made up the heart of the battle.

Throughout Eastview Gardens, beyblade was all the rage. The

anime creators had seen the world wide success of their creation and had cashed in further by creating real beyblades (minus the bit beast sadly), and everyone wanted one. The only issue was these things were extremely expensive and needed to be imported from our neighbor South Africa. However, if there's one thing that Zimbabwean kids are, its innovative. We would use old spray cans, it didn't make a difference if it was a deodorant can, an air freshener can or a bug killer can, all we wanted was the top. We would use a knife to cut the top off, water to clean it and gravel to smooth out the sharp edges.

Once all this was done, we would find a piece of string and wrap it around the top. One would then use a pen barrel to pin the top down, pull the string as hard as they can and boom, your newly made beyblade would spin away.

My group and I each made our own beyblades and would often battle in the halls of Odzi, occasionally entertaining challenges from other Odzi kids. The game quickly replaced open gates as a way to meet new kids and everyone was earnestly having a great time. Everyone but me. Having practiced religiously for days I was already the best at beyblade in my gang, but that wasn't enough.

My little mind had been corrupted by the power of a well placed lie. As I mentioned before, the limitations of my deception were begin to haunt me. I needed to command more influence, but if I dared extend my claims any further than I already had, I would have overplayed my hand. The solution came to me as I was watching an episode of beyblade. The main character was caught in a highly emotional battle, a battle he was losing badly.

Suddenly, like many an anime character before and after him, he called on the power of friendship to save him. Interestingly, it wasn't the power of his actual friends that he called upon, they were watching in horror from the stands (beyblade had entire stadiums dedicated to the sport, hilarious in hindsight). No, our main character called upon his friendship with his bit beast. He begged him to rise up, to fight and win, and fight and win he did. The stadium went wild and in my living room, my friend group went wild too.

Bingo.

"I have a bit beast. That's why I keep winning"

Their heads spun around and they stared daggers at me. I saw betrayal on their faces and knew immediately I had won.

"Oh yeah, he lives in my heart and I'm the only one who can see the beasts, but yeah."

I let this news stew for a short while. Eventually, the question I had been waiting for came. It was Simba who asked,

"How did you get the beast?"

"Oh," I replied, "I had to find a bit beast rock, its hard to tell which one is the right one, but I can tell. If you hit it with your beyblade while your heart is filled with truth and dedication, you can get one too."

Electricity filled the room. Looks of betrayal were quickly replaced by respect and adoration. The "deadly martial art" was nice, but this?! This was the stuff addiction was made of. They begged me to find them rocks. Once again, I became Sensei.

"No my friends. You must go out and find your own rocks. Bring them to me and I will tell you if there is a bit beast inside."

And so it began, the insane search for rocks with bit beasts. They brought me rock after rock and I gave them denial after denial. They would pack rocks they found at school in their school bags, hoping they had finally found their beasts. They would walked around the entirety of the Eastview Gardens, heads bowed low as they searched. Finally, they had each brought the "right" rocks. It was time. We held a little ceremony, each of them stepping up one at a time, rock in hand. They would place the rock on the ground and, with everything they had in them, spin their beyblades and wait in baited silence for the beyblade to strike the rock. I liked the look of quartz, so they had all brought varying sized of crystalline rocks. The best thing about those is, if struck right, they would produce a little spark. The logic I then proposed was the sparks were a symbol of your bit beast entering your heart. To make sure there was no questioning, I made it clear that only I could see the bit beasts and only I could tell their species, in turn only they could name their beasts.

My immature mind saw this as yet another fib, but this was no fib. This was a cruel deception that had permeated society for ages. A deception that has lead to the downfall and rise of entire civilizations and empires. One that is as wildly effective as it is dangerous. In my 9 year old brain I had retained leadership but in reality I had done something truly and deeply disgusting.

I had formed a cult.

Religious Manipulations

I, initially a boy caught in the web of his own lie, inadvertently stumbled upon a powerful tool: the manipulation of faith. His tale echoes throughout history, mirroring the rise and fall of empires built on the shifting sands of religious fanaticism, both harmless and devastating.

The beyblade craze in my friend group, fueled by my "bit beast" power, serves as a chilling small scale display of the manipulation wielded by religious leaders and kings through-out history. While genuine religions have served as guiding lights for humanity, promoting compassion, community, and moral development, the dark side of faith manipulation has bred cults and fostered intolerance, leaving a trail of devastation and societal fractures.

Let's draw a stark line between genuine religious practice, which elevates humanity, and the toxic grip of cults. Across Africa, numerous examples illustrate this stark contrast. On the genuine end, take the Bwiti religion of Gabon, founded in the 19th century. Bwiti emphasizes environmental protection, ancestor veneration, and spiritual communion with nature, fostering a sense of harmony and responsibility within its followers. In stark contrast, the Lord's Resistance Army (LRA), a brutal Ugandan cult led by Joseph Kony, used religion as a tool of control and violence. Kony's warped interpretation of Christianity, infused with mystical pronouncements and exploitation of child soldiers, plunged entire regions into chaos and despair.

Beyond Africa, Europe offers its own cautionary tales. The Crusades, fueled by religious fervor and a thirst for power, unleashed centuries of bloodshed and cultural conflict across the continent. The rise of totalitarian regimes, from Nazi Germany to Soviet Russia, often employed warped ideologies masquerading as religious or secular faiths, resulting in the oppression of dissent and the crushing of individual liberties.

True religions, born from the yearning for meaning and connection, often promote compassion, forgiveness, and the betterment of humankind. Think of Mahatma Gandhi, who weaponized non-violent resistance against colonial oppression, or Desmond Tutu, a beacon of reconciliation in post-apartheid South Africa. Their faith spurred them to fight for justice, equality, and the progress of their communities.

Cults, on the other hand, twist faith into a tool of control. Leaders exploit human vulnerabilities – the desire for belonging, the fear of the unknown and the hunger for purpose. They weave webs of lies, shrouding themselves in mystique and wielding absolute authority. History is littered with such figures: Jim Jones, the leader of the Peoples Temple, who orchestrated the mass suicide of over 900 of his followers in Jonestown on November 18, 1978, or Joseph Smith, whose Mormonism started with claims of buried golden plates and morphed into a powerful religious institution.

The markers of this insidious manipulation are clear:

Charismatic Leadership: Cult leaders project an aura of infallibility. They surround themselves with an air of mystery, demanding unquestioning obedience and fostering a sense of isolation from the outside world.

Exploitation of Vulnerability: Cults prey on individuals seeking solace, purpose, or belonging. They offer simplistic answers to complex questions, promising fulfillment within the confines of their doctrine.

Control of Information: Access to knowledge and external perspectives is restricted. Leaders dictate what is true, often demonizing any dissenting voice, keeping their followers trapped in a bubble of manufactured reality.

Fanaticism, whether religious or secular, fuels the flames of intolerance and conflict. The Rwandan genocide, fueled by ethnic and political divisions exacerbated by religious extremism, serves as a tragic reminder of the destructive potential of unchecked fanaticism. The ongoing tensions in the Middle East, where religious differences are often weaponized by internal and external powers to sow discord and violence, further illustrate the devastating impact of faith-based divisions.

The key to differentiating between genuine religion and manipulative cults lies in their core principles and practices. True religion encourages critical thinking, fosters inclusivity and tolerance, and empowers individuals to make their own choices. In contrast, cults isolate their followers, demand unquestioning obedience, and often exploit their vulnerabilities for personal gain or power.

My "bit beast" charade, though born from childish naivety, high-lights the dangers of blind faith and charismatic manipulation. My childishly constructed web of lies, complete with rituals and pronouncements, created a microcosm of a cult, albeit one confined to the playground of Odzi Court.

So, to bringing all this together, how can you steer clear of the suffocating grip of cults and religious fanaticism?

Seek knowledge and critical thinking. Don't surrender your agency to pronouncements from self-proclaimed prophets. Engage in healthy skepticism, questioning and debating even the most cherished beliefs.

Embrace diversity and tolerance. True faith doesn't demand conformity or demonize different perspectives. Open dialogue and understanding are essential antidotes to the poison of fanaticism.

Remember, leadership based on lies and manipulation, be it on the playground or in the grand theater of history, is a recipe for disaster. The path to a brighter future lies in seeking truth, embracing empathy, and nurturing critical thinking, both within ourselves and in our communities. Only then can we ensure that religion remains a force for good, fostering peace, understanding, and the advancement of humanity, not another tool for control and the descent into darkness.

Ultimately, the true power of faith lies not in unquestioning obedience or fabricated rituals, but in the strength it grants us to face the challenges of life with courage, compassion, and a commitment to building a better world for ourselves and others.

Opposition

After a while (roughly a year), I started to feel less and less of a need to lean on the bit beasts. My friends, though enamored with their imaginary friends, were slowly disassociating their bit beasts from me. The bit beast faze was slowly shifting from "faith" to a game and it quickly became no more than a fun aspect of beyblade. My time as a "priest" was coming to an end and I didn't care.

The martial arts were still pretty solid, but I had now fallen in love with the martial arts themselves and had done away with the deception the training was based on. Training wasn't really compulsory anymore and I only taught those who genuinely wanted to learn. The elasticity of my now 10 year old brain had allowed me to recover from my obsession with leadership and I was entirely focused on having a good time. To be fair, my leadership had gone completely unchallenged for the better part of a year so I was pretty comfortable now. Actually, I was very bored.

Thats when Joshua arrived.

A new family was moving into a second floor apartment and we watched watching silently as the movers carried their property up the stairs. The new comers' home, like my own, overlooked the small field we used to play open gates in, a prime location for sure. Any time a new family moved into our section of Odzi court, we would watch them closely in hopes of spotting a kid our age. Often we were disappointed, but this day we got a new comer, Josh.

From afar, Josh looked like an athletic kid. We knew just by looking at him from that he would be able to keep up with us. Then we saw a DSTV satellite dish being carried to their place and immediately we made the decision to approach him and welcome him to our friend group. As we drew closer to him, we started noticing some additional details. His chin had several scars, an indication that he may be a "naughty kid" and his knuckles were bruised, he was a fighter. When we finally got to him, he greeted us with enthusiasm and exuded incredible charisma. Josh was a leader.

Oddly though, I didn't panic. Josh was an obvious threat to my time as leader, but I was far more curious than I was afraid. If this was a leader, what kind of fun ideas would he bring from where ever he came from? The answer was, plenty! Josh was, as we had deduced, a very naughty kid and with him he brought the world of adrenaline fueled stunts.

"Have you ever jumped from there?" he asked, pointing at the first floor hallway balcony.

We shook our heads in silent unison.

"Watch this."

We watched quietly as Josh ran up the stairs, stood at the edge of the first floor and leaped off of it, landing hard on the grass. He stood up, giggled and ran back up again, only this time we followed. We all climbed over the balcony and looked down. The ground was very far away and I could feel my heart rate going up. I looked at my friends and realized they were all looking at me, waiting. Josh leaped effortlessly and landed on the ground again.He turned back and beckoned us to follow. After a few seconds, I decided cut through the fear and jump.

I landed hard. I lost my balance for a moment, scraping my knees and palms as I tried to sturdy myself. I stood up slowly and stared at my shallow wounds. Then I started giggling. My friends, hearing my elation, immediately jumped too, Tadiwa first and little Paida last. They landed, they all got hurt and they all, like me, loved it! What followed was an Adrenalin craze. We would dare each other to jump from high spots, climb spiraling trees, balance on high beams, taunt the guards and even jump on parked cars. We had no idea what exactly we were doing, but we were slowly perfecting it. We got so good we would start trouble with the guards and then use our daring stunts to escape. Josh taught us to front flip (I was truly awful at it), climb certain walls and leap over small fences. We didn't realize it, but we were doing a kid version of parkour.

Whats truly interesting is, though he was an amazing leader, Josh never once tried to encroach on the things that I led and I gave him the same respect. Josh was also a martial arts student (he studied Kung Fu) and a lot faster in a foot race than I was at this point, but not once did he try to use this to sway anyone. Where beyblade, martial arts, picking the next game or even picking who to hang out with were concerned, I took charge.

But were parkour was concerned, I would step back and let the more experienced and capable Josh take over. We even learned a few new fighting techniques from him and grew to love him as a brother in all aspects our friend group held dear.

Thrive by Embracing Competition

Our friend group, once dominated by my self-styled leadership, transformed into an example of collaboration and mutual respect with the arrival of Joshua. This shift serves as a metaphor for how healthy competition, instead of fostering animosity, can elevate leaders and enrich societies. History offers a treasure trove of examples, proving that embracing the strengths of one's rivals can pave the way for progress and prosperity.

Let us again consider Mansa Musa, the 14th-century emperor of Mali. Renowned for his pilgrimage to Mecca and his subsequent investment in knowledge and cultural exchange, Mansa Musa faced opposition from envious rivals within his own empire. Instead of crushing dissent, he adopted a policy of inclusivity, incorporating capable rivals into his administration and harnessing their expertise for the betterment of Mali. By recognizing the potential within his opponents, Mansa Musa solidified his own leadership and ushered in a golden age of Malian prosperity.

Across the continent, in Rwanda, a nation scarred by genocide, Paul Kagame rose to power with a mission of reconciliation and unity. Despite facing internal resistance from extremists,

Kagame prioritized national healing over retribution. He fostered a cabinet diverse in ethnicity and political opinion, promoting dialogue and inclusivity instead of stoking the flames of division. While challenges remain, Rwanda's remarkable progress in the aftermath of the genocide stands as a testament to the power of embracing competing voices in the pursuit of a common goal.

The secret sauce of these leaders lies in their ability to differentiate between ego and the needs of the greater good. They understand that true leadership involves drawing strength from a constellation of voices, not just the echo of their own. Leaders who view their rivals as enemies to be crushed are ultimately crippled by self-doubt and insecurity. In contrast, those who embrace healthy competition create an environment where diverse perspectives clash and spark innovation, leaving room for growth and shared successes.

The corporate landscape has also witnessed leaders who, by embracing competition, propelled their organizations to unprecedented heights. Take, for instance, the tech industry, where the rivalry between Microsoft and Apple during the late 20th century revolutionized personal computing.

In the 1980s and 1990s, Microsoft, led by Bill Gates, and Apple, under Steve Jobs, engaged in fierce competition for dominance in the computer market. Gates, recognizing the potential of graphical user interfaces, collaborated with Apple to develop software for Macintosh computers. This strategic move not only showcased healthy competition but also marked a turning point in the industry, laying the groundwork for modern operating systems.

Similarly, in the realm of e-commerce, the rivalry between Amazon and eBay has reshaped online retail. Jeff Bezos, the founder of Amazon, recognized the strengths of eBay's auction model but sought to create a more customer-centric platform. The competition between the two giants fueled innovation, resulting in improved services, faster delivery, and enhanced user experiences for consumers worldwide.

Moving to the automobile industry, the competition between Tesla and traditional automakers, like General Motors (GM) and Ford, has accelerated the adoption of electric vehicles. Elon Musk's Tesla disrupted the market by focusing on electric cars, compelling traditional automakers to invest heavily in electric vehicle technology. This healthy competition has not only expanded the electric vehicle market but has also pushed the entire industry toward sustainability.

These examples illustrate that healthy competition, when embraced by leaders, becomes a catalyst for innovation, growth, and shared successes. Leaders who recognize the strengths of their competitors, as demonstrated by Mansa Musa and Paul Kagame, create environments where diverse perspectives clash and spark innovation.

In the corporate world, this clash of ideas and strengths results in breakthrough products, improved services, and a more dynamic marketplace. Instead of viewing competitors as enemies to be crushed, successful leaders identify the good in their rivals, fostering a culture of collaboration and adaptation.

The dynamic between Joshua and I exemplifies this principle.

Though competitors for leadership, we recognized each other's strengths and created a symbiotic relationship. Secure in my role as game master and Sensei, I had no issues allowing Joshua's parkour expertise to shine, even going as far as letting him be a Sensei too. This mutual respect not only fostered a stronger, more diverse friend group but also allowed both of us to blossom into more well-rounded leaders.

The lesson extends beyond the playground. We must reject the zero-sum games of political, corporate and social discourse, where victory requires the crushing of all dissent. Instead, we must embrace the richness of diverse perspectives, fostering environments where healthy competition becomes a catalyst for collective progress. Leaders who can identify the good in their rivals, who can listen, learn, and adapt, are those who will ultimately guide us towards a brighter future.

Let us remember that the rose thrives not in isolation, but in a garden teeming with competitors. It is through the constant struggle for sunlight and water that its petals unfurl in their glory. In the same way, it is through competing ideas and differing strengths that societies flourish and leaders truly rise to their potential.

It Smells Like Rain

Our small friend group was finally doing well. Granted we were quite naughty now, but we had never been closer as friends, as brothers. My more positive attributes were shining bright now that my ego was in check and we were so well resourced and entertained that life was, like the song, a breeze. This wouldn't last long though. Clouds were gathering in the distance. Trouble was brewing. In our escapades and training we had gone far beyond Odzi, displaying our strength and power to all the other courts. 6 courts, smaller than Odzi, but still massive. Numerous groups of ambitious kids with leaders, skills and needs of their own had watched us. They had grown to respect us, then fear us, and now some deeply despised us.

War was coming, and much like the Trojan debacle of legend, it would be triggered by a scandalous love affair.

4

Beyond Personal Gain

Her name was Rumbidzai, and I was crazy about her. The first time I saw her, we were at school. I didn't think too much of her then because there were plenty of pretty girls at school, so she didn't quite stand out; not until she smiled.

Rumbi had one of those genuine, wide, toothy smiles that made you feel appreciated, even if you saw it from across the room. I caught her smiling at a mutual friend and as soon as she was out of eye shot, I approached the friend and insisted she introduce us. She wasn't in my class so we had to wait the whole day for school to end before any introductions could be made. I thought myself a a real charmer (I had dated 2 whole girls after all), so confidence wasn't an issue, I just needed the perfect opening line.

Finally, school ended and my friend told me to wait in the hockey field. I sprinted to the field and waited impatiently. Finally, they showed up, and she smiled again. All my lines, my smoothness, my suave and charm went right out the window and I just gazed at her with a goofy grin on my face.

"Hi," she said confidently.

I licked my dry lips, nodded and kept smiling.

"Aaron, right?"

I nodded slowly, swaying from side to side and rubbing my hands slowly. What the hell was I doing?! I needed to salvage this quickly.

"Want some of my left over sandwich?" I muttered.

What was that?! My friend, mortified, shook her head and walked away. Rumbi giggled and nodded.

"Sure"

We sat and shared what was left of my egg sandwich as my confidence slowly returned. I was tempted to refer back to my dark deceptions to win her heart, but something about that felt deeply wrong. Instead, Rumbi met neither the Sensei nor the Priest, she just met normal old Aaron, and she liked him. I started walking her home and it didn't even dawn on me that we were headed toward Eastview Gardens. By the time I realized, we were at the complex gate. I hid my face from the guards (parkour had made me a wanted man) and made sure Rumbi didn't notice my clandestine efforts. A girl like her might not like a naughty kid.

When we were inside, we continued our conversations as we drifted slowly toward her court. We were so engaged in our talk, I didn't realize were we were until she stopped and said,

"Okay, this is where I live. You can't come too close , but thanks for walking me."

Finally, with the spell broken I looked up and realized we were at Mupfure court, and I was in deep trouble.

You see, like I mentioned before, there were 7 courts at Eastview Gardens. Odzi, Manyame, Ngezi, Bhubhi, Gwai, Zambezi and Mupfure. Most of these courts had fairly normal kids, but 2 of them had kids that ventured beyond naughty, and landed firmly in dangerous. Those courts were Ngezi and Mupfure, with Ngezi being neutral chaotic and Mupfure being aggressively chaotic. Beyond aggression, Mupfure had high numbers of tough kids despite the building's relatively small size. They were united in a way no other court was and they would use their numbers to demolish anyone who stood in their way. A few months prior, rumors had spread that Mupfure had subdued and absorbed the Zambezi gang by force, an occurrence that was entirely unheard of. These kids were conquerors, a very real danger.

The Mupfure kids were lead by a boy named Scar. It wasn't his real name, but when you have that many scars on your body, you earn a fitting moniker. Scar was a ruthless bully. I had never had reason to confront Scar because he never ventured outside of his territory and my boys knew better than to approach Mupfure. In that way, Scar and I had a tentative peace agreement. You stick to your territory, I stick to mine. Yet, here I was, standing on Mupfure lawn, with a Mupfure girl, hugging.

Wait, was she hugging me? Awesome!

Suddenly, I heard a whistle in the distance. I didn't even need to look to figure out that one of Scar's scouts had spotted me. Rumbi's body language changed immediately.

"You have to go, Scar likes me and if he sees you he will hurt you."

This had just gotten far worse than venturing beyond my territory, this had just become a love triangle. Panic engulfed me, my mouth went dry and I had never felt fear that potent. I nodded and sprinted as fast as I could back to Odzi. I rushed into the house, shut the door and sat on the couch, struggling to catch my breath. My mind was moving at a million miles an hour. Scar was a massive danger, but Rumbi was so amazing. Was this potential relationship worth the trouble it would bring. The answer washed over me like a calming wave.

Yes. This was 100% worth it.

For the next month, I walked Rumbi from school half way to Mupfure daily. On weekends, I would go to Rumbi's house to hang out, but never alone. I would always go with Tadiwa and Number 2 as body guards in case of trouble. On a couple of occasions I spotted Scar himself watching us from afar, but he never approached us directly or tried anything. I took this as a sign that he didn't actually care as much as I had initially assumed and continued to woo Rumbi. She wasn't my girlfriend on any official terms, but boys had started staying away from her out of respect. The peace was tentative, but somewhat stable. Or at least it was until the first day of the school holiday.

On the last day of school we always got a half day. School finished at 11am and as always, Rumbi and I walked hometogether. As usual, after leaving her before reaching Mupfure, I skipped back to Odzi. Before I even got to Odzi, I saw Paida sprinting as fast as he could toward me. He seemed terrified and by the time he reached me he was completely out of breath.

"They….They got…They got…"

"Slowly kid," I said as I rubbed his back.

"They got Josh. Mupfure got Josh."

You know, to this day there are a handful of events that truly sent a shiver down my spine. This may have been the very first one.

According to Paida, he and Josh had got home about an hour ago. They changed quickly and decided to go for a run. In my absence, Josh was Sensei and he was as serious about training as I was. As a precaution, I had told the boys not to jog past Mupfure anymore, so we had an alternate path that used the Gwai hallways, which were still fairly close to Mupfure, but far enough away for the boys to remain clandestine. Apparently they weren't clandestine enough, because Mupfure had figured out our new path and had laid in wait. Six Mupfure boys had emerged from some bushes and ambushed Paida and Josh. Josh, being the noble leader he was, had instructed little Paida to run away whilst he held the Mupfure boys back. Paida had initially refused, choosing instead to fight beside his brother in arms, but then they started to get overwhelmed. Josh's noble gesture turned into an order, one Paida could not refuse and Paida had ran away as fast as he could. Turning back from a safe distance, Paida had witnessed the Mupfure boys starting to lose to Josh and then start to use stones instead of fists. Josh had ran away and the last Paida saw of him, he was being chased whilst being pelted with stones.

I was frozen. Every bit of fear I had felt of the Mupfure boys was melted away by pure rage. How dare they attack my boys. How dare they come after us so brazenly. I had to retaliate. The Mupfure boys would regret ever messing with us!

We ran back to Odzi and I ordered Paida to fetch everyone whilst I went to check on Josh. I went toward Josh's house and found him by a tap, outside, washing his wounds. He had managed to make it home bruised and battered, but okay. As soon as he saw me, tears welled up in his eyes. We said nothing to each other. Instead we stood face to face, tears in both our eyes. This disrespect would not stand. Finally, Paida arrived with the rest of the gang.

"Sensei we are ready!," I heard Number 2 yell.

I turned around and looked at my friends. Tadiwa, Number 2, Simba, Dereck and Paida looked back at me. They were ready to go to war, win or lose they were ready to fight. Looking at them though, reality began to set in. The Mupfure gang alone was made up of at least 30 kids, add to that the 12 or so Zambezi gang kids they had assimilated and we were thoroughly outnumbered. Sending 6 kids to attack Josh was no coincidence. Scar was showing me how badly outnumbered we were. In a direct confrontation we would be badly beaten. Even if we tried ambushes, these savages never ventured far from each other. Recruiting all the Odzi kids would still not be enough, they were numerous but very inexperienced, untrained. To give in to rage now would put my boys in even more danger. No. We had to think bigger.

Mupfure had assimilated Zambezi through brute force, bullying them into subservience. That was not our way, but… the core concept of assimilation was genius. Every court had at least one gang that had copied our training traditions. If we developed a new method of taking over other courts, we could gather an army of moderately to well trained kids that would rival, or even overshadow, the Mupfure forces. To wage this war, I had to win a lot more victories. We would start with the weakest courts, then move on to our most powerful rivals.

This war wasn't just Odzi vs Mupfure anymore, this had just become the Eastview war, and it would be epic.

Navigating the Minefield of Conflict

My encounter with Rumbi and the subsequent clash with Scar's Mupfure gang transforms Eastview Gardens into an example of the complex dance between peace and conflict that has shaped human history. From my young self's adventures, we gain a narrative that offers a lens through which to examine the motivations for war, the consequences of choosing conflict over diplomacy, and the delicate balance between individual needs and the collective good.

Throughout history, countless leaders have faced similar quandaries. Mahatma Gandhi, confronted by the seemingly insurmountable might of the British Empire, chose the path of non-violent resistance, wielding empathy and moral force as his weapons. His unwavering commitment to peace proved surprisingly effective, ultimately breaking the colonial yoke and inspiring generations of activists. Gandhi's non-violent resistance against the British Empire in the early 20th century serves as a poignant example of how peaceful means can effectively challenge oppressive forces. His advocacy for civil disobedience and non-cooperation showcased the power of moral force, leading to India's eventual independence in 1947.

Contrastingly, the conquests of Alexander the Great in the 4th century BCE and Napoleon Bonaparte's military campaigns in the late 18th and early 19th centuries underscore the destructive consequences of unchecked ambition. While Alexander's vast empire stretched from Greece to India, his relentless pursuit of conquest led to the suffering of countless communities caught in the wake of his armies. Similarly, Napoleon's quest for European dominance resulted in widespread warfare, leaving behind a trail of destruction and reshaping the geopolitical landscape.

The decision to wage war is rarely a simple one, often fueled by a combination of factors beyond mere personal ego. Economic interests, territorial disputes, ideological clashes, and resource scarcity can all act as triggers, pushing nations towards conflict. Even within smaller communities, like Eastview Gardens, rivalries and perceived injustices can escalate into violence, as Scar's brutal attack on Josh demonstrates.

However, the cost of war, both human and societal, is often borne, not by those who lead armies and issue pronouncements, but by the ordinary citizens caught in the crossfire. Families are torn apart, economies crumble, and entire regions become battlegrounds, often for causes they barely understand. The scars of war, like Josh's physical wounds, are a stark reminder of the fragility of peace and the devastating consequences of choosing conflict over dialogue.

My initial rage at the Mupfure attack on Josh was a visceral reaction to the harm inflicted on my friend. Yet, I took a critical moment to pause, to assess the situation rationally. Recognizing the overwhelming odds against us, I chose a different path: not an immediate confrontation, but a strategic campaign of expansion and alliance-building.

This strategy mirrors real-world examples of empire-building through conquest and alliance. The Roman Republic, through a combination of military might and strategic alliances, rose to dominate the Mediterranean world. Similarly, Genghis Khan, by uniting disparate Mongol tribes and forging strategic alliances, created a vast empire that stretched across Asia.

However, history also offers cautionary tales of empires built on brute force and fear. The Assyrian Empire, notorious for its brutality and cruelty, ultimately met its demise due to internal rebellions and external pressures. Similarly, Napoleon Bonaparte's ambitious military campaigns, while initially successful, eventually led to his defeat and exile, underscoring the pitfalls of unchecked ambition and military aggression.

The Eastview Gardens war might be a playground skirmish, but the lessons it carries resonate far beyond the confines of childhood. It reminds us that the choice between peace and war is not always clear-cut, but it is a choice we must make nonetheless. By learning from history, both grand and small, and prioritizing empathy and understanding over violence and aggression, we can hope to build a future where playgrounds and nations alike remain places of laughter and joy, not battlegrounds of ambition and hate.

The Sun Sets on Peace

There was a part of Odzi, on the fourth floor, near Number 2's place, where you could see most of Eastview gardens. Around sunset, I went up there to think. I had inspired the gang, but war was no small thing. We had never used our skills offensively before and if this campaign went badly there was a real chance that Odzi would just emerge with way more enemies than friends. There was absolutely no room for failure and that pressure fell squarely on my shoulders. I looked out at the other courts and began trying to figure out the perfect order of attack and how to take down each unique opponent. Mupfure had started this war, but the responsibility of ending it was now mine.

Number 2 walked up and stood beside me. He too looked across the land. Number 2 was a living defiance of the "big and dumb" stereotype. He was the wisest of my gang and I often leaned on his advice and calming demeanor in trying times.

"You sure about all this Sensei?" he asked after a while.

We stood there quietly for a moment. I had the beginnings of a plan ready and I was running possible outcomes in my juvenile head.

"I'm sure we are going to win."

Number 2 turned to face me. He analyzed my face and put a hand on my shoulder.

"Aaron, I trust you, we all trust you, but we could get hurt doing this, even if we win. This could all go really wrong. All this over a girl? Are you sure about this?"

I sighed. "Bro, this isn't about Rumbi. I won't even be seeing her anymore."

I wasn't kidding. Rumbi and I never really spoke again after Josh got attacked. We would see each other a few times at school in months to come but she had become a reminder of my selfishness and irresponsibility, so things were never the same. Eventually she moved to another neighborhood and school entirely and by then, I barely noticed.

"Truth is," I continued, "this is all really scary. Scar is a serious problem and no one is doing anything about it. Now he is attacking us and hurting our friends. Josh helped Paida, but imagine if Paida had been alone. I was there when Jacob hurt that kid so bad he had to get surgery. I did nothing to help him. Now, I get to choose if we live in fear forever or free ourselves. I failed the first time I had to help my little brother, I just can't fail again especially now that all of my brothers could get hurt."

Number 2 nodded and turned back to survey the land.

"Alright boss, where do we start?"

5

The Cost of Valor

I devised very simple rules of war. We would approach the most powerful gang of each court and challenge them. They could either engage us in a fighting competition, a beyblade tournament or both. If they refused or if the competitions ended in a draw, we would regard them as a neutral party in our war. If we lost, we would be assimilated into their gang and submit to their leadership. But if we won, they would become part of Odzi's forces and submit to our leadership indefinitely.

Our training regiment went through the roof. Now we had to incorporate beyblade into our training . I told the boys that to make their bit beasts stronger they needed to train at least twice a day. To eliminate weakness in our beyblading, we had to devise a new way to launch our beyblades, so instead of using a barrel, which slowed us down, we would launch from the air. We started a regiment of daily martial arts sparring and daily beyblade launching training that consisted of each of us launching our beyblades at bricks until the brick cracked in half. It was grueling, painful work.

But such is the price of war.

First on our campaign trail was Bhubhi court. Not much was known about Bhubhi, except that it was the smallest court in all of Eastview and by extension, had the smallest gang. I wasn't going to go in blind regardless, so we watched them for a full afternoon before we made our approach. They did not seem to have a leader, just an adult chaperon, which was new to us but not unheard of. Their prime gang hardly hung out together to train, which seemed rather odd, but I figured that would make things a lot easier.

Bhubhi was an absolute necessity because it was located right in the middle of Eastview gardens. It also overlooked the jungle gym and had some of the most interesting hill-like terrain, perfect for endurance training. If we got Bhubhi, we could watch other courts and also have any gangs we conquered come train here in relative safety. The jungle gyms would expand our possibilities where calisthenics were concerned too. The cherry on top was Josh's parents had decided to move to Bhubhi for its cheaper rentals (and also possibly because they didn't like us all that much, but that's an overestimation of our influence on such a serious decision). Bhubhi simply made sense, it was the perfect first move.

Finally, the day came when we approached Bhubhi. We were now on holiday so we had the whole day to dedicate to negotiations. The Bhubhi gang saw us coming and assembled to intercept us. There weren't a lot of them, but they seemed slightly bigger than we had expected. Older too. We met them in the road and laid down our terms.

"How many fights?," one of the Bhubhi kids piped up.

"How many do you want?," I retorted.

The Bhubhi kids mumbled among themselves.

"One, you fight our leader tomorrow. Today we do beyblade."

That caught us by surprise. Our investigations had indicated they did not have a leader. The fact that they chose to have one fight, knowing exactly how capable we all were, was also quite concerning. We were missing something.

"Who is your leader?"

Suddenly, a deep voice boomed from behind us, "I am."

We turned around, only to find the chaperon we had spied watching the Bhubhi kids towering over us. His name was Brian and he was 16 years old. He was so large compared to us that we had assumed he was an adult, and frankly he may as well have been! We had been completely blind sided. I had foolishly assigned too little time to our investigations, forcing us to rush a conflict that ended up being a trap and now we were about to pay for it. My gang was starting to panic and I could see their resolve breaking. We still had a beyblade match to win, so panic was unacceptable.

"Okay," I said as I walked up to Brian. I looked him up and down and then made eye contact with the giant and crossed my arms defiantly, "time and place."

I could feel Bhubhi's confusion from behind me. For a moment, even Brian's confidence faltered. Then he laughed.

"You can't fight me alone kid, I will fight two of you."

I maintained eye contact still. "Okay, time and place."

My gang's confidence was starting to return as they watched their leader face down this enormous threat. In truth, I was scared out of my mind. Brian was fairly skinny, but we all were! He also happened to have years of puberty fueled growth and was undoubtedly stronger than us. 2 of us simply would not be enough, worse still, who among my brothers was I going to sentence to join me in this futile suicide mission?

"2pm, tomorrow at Odzi on the 3rd floor by the right side elevators," he said menacingly.

"Okay," I said with a nonchalant shrug, "now let's beyblade."

My gang clapped loudly and cheered as I stepped back from the face off. The beyblade tournament went great. Our new strategy of air launching worked perfectly and our training showed, we won every single match up with little to no effort. Bhubhi seemed to be having fun though. They didn't have a single worry in the world. You wouldn't either if you had a giant in your ranks. As I watched my brothers demolish the

Bhubhi gang, I stood haunted by my grave miscalculation. I knew I was going to get hurt tomorrow, but the degree to which I got injured could be lessened by having someone else there to help. Only issue was, they would get hurt too. Considering this insanity started because one among our ranks got hurt, was this war worth that happening over and over again? This was literally only the beginning! I couldn't make anyone fight Brian, this was my responsibility and I would take it on like the leader I had pretended to be.

The next day, I woke up quite late and went for solitary training. I did my usual routine and avoided my friends the entire time. Finally, the time for us to fight was approaching. I went upstairs alone, sat in the chosen battle ground and waited. I did my best to channel Bruce Lee from that one fight he had with Chuck Norris, stretching awkwardly and taking deep breaths whilst tensing my muscles.

"We have been looking for you bro," Tadiwa said, appearing quietly from around a corner.

He was alone and he walked up to me then sat next to me.

"I know what you are thinking bro, you won't fight him alone. We will do this tog…"

"No," I said quietly, "Josh was hurt because of me. Paida was almost hurt because of me, I won't let you be hurt because of me."

Tadiwa tilted his head slightly and smiled.

"This isn't about you anymore bro. This is about Scar. Yes, Rumbi was a bad idea, but there was also no way Scar was going to stop at Zambezi. Scar will come after all of us unless we stop him. If you fight alone, you might lose and then what? We draw and lose the jungle gym, the position and the hills because you are scared?"

Tadiwa had never been this brutally vocal. I felt disrespected and lashed out immediately.

"I'm about to fight this guy alone, how am I scared Tadiwa. Are you challenging me?"

Tadiwa sat up straight. "I don't care if you are scared of Brian, but I do know you are scared of letting us help you. That fear is going to lose us this war and Scar will take over Eastview. I don't care if you hate me man, but I am fighting Brian too, not because of you, but because we need to win."

Tadiwa's words cut deep. I felt responsible for this situation starting (justifiably) and I was letting that guilt force me into making foolish decisions that would put everyone in even more danger. Not just everyone in Odzi, but the whole of Eastview. I had, by starting this campaign, become responsible for far more than my own pride and guilty conscience. My friends needed me to be humble, decisive and clear minded. Tadiwa was here for himself and the people he cares about, just like I was. He, and everyone else, deserved a chance to survive the black tide of Mupfure.

I started to cry.

"We don't have to win, we just have to not lose." I said, a sheepish smile developing on my tear soaked face.

Tadiwa understood immediately.

Suddenly we heard footsteps approaching, Brian was coming. I hurriedly wiped my face and stood up with Tadiwa's help. We stood there, waiting for our foe to appear. Finally, from the shade across the hall, Brian emerged. He looked bigger somehow, and his face was set in stone. There would be no mercy from him today. Good, because we wanted none. The plan was simple, Brian was bigger than us but completely unskilled. He was also quite unfit, despite his slender physique. The fight could only be concluded by catastrophic loss (can't fight anymore) or forfeit; no time limits, which meant if we kept going long enough, Brian might get tired of beating us up and we could secure our victory. Brian regarded us for a moment and then threw a punch at my face. I was taken by surprise and barely dodged. The fight was on.

For the next 20 minutes, Tadiwa and I took turns battling Brian. Each time I grew tired or got hurt, I would quickly retreat and let Tadiwa step in and he would do the same, allowing me to return to the battle. In earnest, we barely even scratched Brian. We kicked his legs a lot and grappled a bit, but he was pummeling us continuously and we were doing our best to absorb the hits. It was brutal, but it was also working. Brian was starting to breath heavy and taking a knee each time Tadiwa and I traded places. The strikes to his legs had actually been significant! Tadiwa and I were also exhausted, but our training had taught us to keep pushing regardless.

Finally, Brian made a fatal mistake, he took a little too long on his knees during our switch and simultaneously lost focus on us. I jumped on his back and put him in a choke hold. Tadiwa, seeing the opening, jumped in and did everything in his power to hold Brian's hands down. Brian tried to get up, but our weight kept him off center so he fell down. Now on the ground, in a choke hold and unable to effectively defend himself, the big guy was in a serious bind.

"Okay Okay," he croaked, "I quit. You win."

The Double-Edged Sword of Valor

My journey from reckless freedom fighter to strategic leader reflects the complex dance between individual bravery and collective responsibility that every leader, from playground warriors to presidents, must navigate.

One of the most striking aspects of my initial approach was my willingness to throw myself into the fray, to face the formidable Brian alone. This display of personal courage, while commendable, was ultimately rooted in a dangerous self-reliance. I shouldered the burden of responsibility entirely, fueled by a desire to protect my friends and a lingering guilt over Josh's injury. This self-inflicted pressure blinded me to the power of collaboration and nearly led me to a disastrous encounter with Brian.

Tadiwa's intervention serves as a crucial turning point. He

challenged my self-imposed martyrdom, reminding me that leadership encompasses more than just personal valor. It demands the ability to delegate, to trust and rely on others, and to recognize that individual sacrifice, while noble, might not always be the most effective course of action.

This realization dawned on me as I reflected on the wider implications of my actions. This war wasn't just about Rumbi and I anymore; it was about protecting all of Eastview Gardens from the tyranny of Scar. This broadened perspective compelled me to re-evaluate our strategy, embracing collaboration, forging an alliance with Tadiwa to face Brian.

History offers numerous examples of leaders who, learned the value of collaboration through hard-won experience. Winston Churchill, initially known for his impetuous nature, eventually understood the importance of building alliances and seeking counsel, leading Britain to victory against Nazi Germany. Similarly, Abraham Lincoln, despite facing internal dissent during the Civil War, recognized the critical role of compromise and negotiation in uniting the nation.

However, the pendulum must swing both ways. While blind self-sacrifice is detrimental, so too is an aloof leadership detached from the struggles of its people. Many times in history, leaders who were willing to sacrifice themselves have formed the heart of movements and freedom fighting efforts. Nelson Mandela, a symbol of selfless resistance against apartheid, understood the importance of leading from the front, sharing the hardships and dangers faced by his followers. Mahatma Gandhi's non-violent campaigns relied heavily on his own willingness to endure hunger, imprisonment, and physical assault, demonstrating the power of personal leadership by example.

The true challenge lies in finding the delicate balance between these two extremes. A leader must be courageous and decisive, able to face challenges head-on, but also wise enough to recognize when collaboration is key. They must inspire trust and delegate responsibility, while remaining grounded in the realities and sacrifices shared by their people.

For me, the fight against Scar was just beginning. Gwai, Ngezi and Manyame would present new challenges and opportunities for me to hone my leadership skills. I had to learn to embrace both the strength of individual valor and the power of collective action, ensuring that our ambition to protect Eastview Gardens was not fueled by personal glory, but by the well-being of all its inhabitants.

The playground, like the world, demands leaders who are not simply brave warriors, but strategic thinkers, capable of inspiring and uniting, of recognizing their own limitations and leveraging the strengths of those around them. Only then can they navigate the complex landscape of leadership, where personal valor finds its true meaning in the collective fight for a just and equitable future.

A Battle Won, as War Continues

Tadiwa and I couldn't believe it! We looked at each other and immediately started bawling. We embraced and cry-laughed for what felt like ages. Finally, we went downstairs with Brian in tow. Both Bhubhi and Odzi were gathered downstairs; not just the main gangs, but a lot of kids from Odzi and a lot of kids from Bhubhi. News of this insane fight had traveled like wildfire, I even spotted a kid from Ngezi and another from Manyame in the crowd; spies no doubt. Good, I wanted them to see this.

Brian's legs still hurt and the walking was too much for him, so as soon as he got to the curb, he sat down and rested his head on his knees. This made for the perfect image as both Tadiwa and I stood over him and held our hands high. The reactions varied. Odzi cheered, Bhubhi was stunned and the spies ran off as quickly as they could (likely to report these events to their leaders).

Bhubhi was bummed, but they were now part of the movement to stop Scar and I needed them inspired. Brain finally managed to stand up and I put my hand on his shoulder and smiled. He smiled back and nodded in respect, a gesture that lead to a few smiles breaking out among the Bhubhi gang.

"Bhubhi," I said, channeling my most convincing 'King voice', "From now on you are our brothers. We will train together, play together and protect all of Eastview gardens together. Welcome to the family."

The cheers were a bit restrained, but universal this time. Our first hurdle had been conquered and I had learned a powerful lesson; we were all in this together. We still needed a lot more more people to "together" with though.

So on to the next. Gwai Court.

6

Information as Power

Mupfure had heard about the battle of Bhubhi and now they found themselves in a weird position. They still had us on numbers thanks to their court's population of violent kids and their recent acquisition of the similarly populated Zambezi court, but the threat we posed was growing. They needed to make a move and quickly. Thing was, the only courts left were Gwai, Ngezi and Manyame.

Gwai was a ridiculously underpopulated court where kids our age were concerned. The place was just a bunch of toddlers and parents, with maybe one or two 7 year olds. Basically, Gwai wouldn't bolster anyone's numbers. Then there was Ngezi and Manyame. Both courts were ruled by insane leaders who had a penchant for violence. Ngezi and Manyeme used to fight each other for fun. This might sound a lot like how Odzi came up, but let me be clear, their fights were **brutal**.

So Scar's options were to either take over a useless court (Gwai) or risk weakening his position by attacking Manyame or Mupfure. The latter option was tough because Mupfure was a blunt instrument. They lacked the fineness required to create fair terms in battle and instead preferred to ambush their opponents and break them as quickly as possible. Manyame and Ngezi would not break easy, hence why Mupfure found themselves in this weird position.

Back at Odzi, we weren't quite stuck, in fact we had a very clear plan. What Scar had failed to recognize was, even though Gwai was under populated, the court was right across the road from both Mupfure and Zambezi (which were next to each other). Information was power in this battle and we needed a solid vantage point from which we could spy on Mupfure. Better still, Gwai's back yard lead to a path that gave direct access to both Bhubhi and Ngezi. Gwai may have had no real personnel value where fighting was concerned, but it definitely had great strategic potential.

There was no point challenging Gwai to a fight or even a beyblade match, besides those activities would be too visible. Our best approach, then, was to make friends with one of the 7 year olds, preferably one who lived on the ground floor. The ground floor flats in all of East View Gardens didn't have railings on their back verandas, an advantage we needed for ease of movement. I took this task upon myself, identifying the perfect kid to ally with and approaching him whilst he was busy with his toys.

"Hey, whats up? I'm Aaron, whats your name?"

The kid turned, regarded me suspiciously and then turned back to his toys. He might have been 7, but he was not an idiot. He knew exactly who I was and probably assumed he knew why I was there.

"I don't want to fight."

"No," I said gently, "I don't want to fight either. I want to stop Scar."

"Why?"

"Um…because he is bad?" I said a bit confused.

"Not to me" he responded nonchalantly.

I wasn't quite prepared for this. Most kids hated Scar because he was a bully and a serious threat. Gwai had absolutely no reason to hate Scar. In fact, their proximity to Mupfure meant other bully types generally stayed away from them and their low numbers meant Scar had no interest in them whatsoever. I had come to offer freedom to a kid who, in reality, was the most free of us all. Gwai was happy to be neutral because everyone left them alone!

That's it!

"Oh that's cool, you and your friends must be real happy about that."

The kid stopped playing for a moment. He turned around and stared daggers at me.

"I don't have friends."

I nodded and kissed my lips, feigning pity. I walked up to him, grabbed a toy car and started moving it about on the stone veranda.

"I have plenty. I have friends at Bhubhi and even more at Odzi."

The kid saw right through me, but was tempted regardless.

"I'm not allowed to go that far."

"We can come to you."

"Tashinga."

I stopped playing with the little car and looked up at our new ally. Tashinga, a solid name for a solid kid.

"You have to come over a lot to play games with me. I have a PS2" he said excitedly.

This was perfect! Some of the gang had off-brand gaming stations but no one had a Play Station 2! Convincing everyone to hang out with Tashinga was going to be a lot easier than I had initially thought!

For the next week, the focus became spying. At Bhubhi, which was fairly close to Ngezi and partially opposite the sprawling Manyame court (Manyame was a floor shorter that Odzi but was the only court that rivaled it in length and population), the

Bhubhi kids would go "visit" their neighbors and watch their activities. Meanwhile at Gwai, a few Odzi civilians and I would go to Tashinga's house through the veranda door and hang out while playing video games. His parents didn't mind, in fact they loved how popular their kid suddenly was. While the others played, I would go outside and watch Mupfure and Zambezi, trying to get an idea of what was going on over there. Additionally, I had been gifted roller skates by a kind neighbor and my lieutenants and I took turns using them to move around quickly throughout the inner paths of Eastview and the corridors at individual courts for information distribution.

The spy network was thriving.

The following are the results of our spy missions.

Mupfure:

- Scar seemed to be keeping most activities out of sight, however some of his troops had been seen training. They were practicing both beyblade and martial arts.
- Some Zambezi troops were unhappy with their Mupfure overlords.
- Mupfure had a small thicket area near the road that they used to guard their territory unseen and ambush any trespassers
- There were some new kids, one of whom looked particularly rich

Ngezi:

- The court was run by a guy named Hussein (a complex situation which will be made clear in the Manyame section). Hussein was brutal in battle and incredibly naughty, but was also a really kind leader beloved by his people.
- Ngezi had greater numbers than we initially assumed.
- they had several bikes, a great asset for moving quickly around the courts
- Hussein had gotten his people into sparring based martial arts early and would play "sword" games with thin metal bars they had found in the rubbish dumps. They were quite skilled
- Hussein's gang did not beyblade

Manyame:

- The court was run by a girl named Nyasha. I knew Nyasha from Kindergarten and she was one of the few girls I had "dated" at this point in my life (it was never official but we held hands a bunch, which counts)
- Nyasha had a pretty solid gang with lots of martial arts training
- Manyame had taken over Ngezi, allowing Hussein to remain in charge, but having the court serve as an extension of Manyame. Apparently Nyasha had challenged Hussein to a one on one exhibition of skill, then manipulated him into competing in skills he was awful at, thus winning. This was somewhat unofficial but understood to be true.
- Nyasha had grown to be quite muscular. Reports indicated she was even stronger than me and Number 2.
- Nyasha placed no importance on beyblade, however her gang played beyblade casually.

- The Manyame gang was skilled in fighting with metal bars in the sword game too.
- Nyasha also had roller skates, only hers weren't inline like mine, they were outdoor skates (2 rows of 2 wheels), allowing for a shorter learning period for new skaters.

All of this was vital information from which a strategy could be created. Additionally, Josh's parents had made good on their move and he now lived at Bhubhi. He became the leader there and I had him coordinate efforts and watch over the court. Bhubhi was fairly laid back, so most of it was fun and games, but they were also very effective.

We were in the best position possible to win this war. Everything just had to go perfect.

The Art of War

The establishment of the information network that we used to gain intel on our future conquests creates a valuable lens through which to examine the critical role of information in leadership and conflict resolution. As much as we were playing at real life with childish battle, the strategies we employed, both consciously and unconsciously warrant a closer look.

Scar's reliance on brute force and ambushes, fuelled by inaccurate intel, left him vulnerable. He underestimated the value of Gwai's strategic location and failed to grasp the simmering discontent within Zambezi, both crucial details unearthed by our astute spy network.

This isn't just a playground phenomenon. Consider the 2008 financial crisis, where Wall Street giants, armed with inaccurate financial models and flawed risk assessments, made disastrous bets, plunging the world into economic turmoil. Similarly, the failed launch of New Coke in 1985 by Coca-Cola stemmed from a misreading of consumer preferences, leading to a massive public backlash and a hasty return to the original formula.

But information gathering isn't solely about outsmarting the enemy. Understanding the needs and motivations of allies is equally crucial. My childish diplomacy with Gwai, recognizing their neutrality stemmed not from fear but from contentment, underscores this point. Leaders seeking to build alliances and navigate complex social dynamics must recognize and cater to diverse perspectives and motivations.

This echoes the leadership of Patagonia founder Yvon Chouinard. Instead of prioritizing shareholder returns, Chouinard understood the concerns of environmental activists and employees, transferring ownership of his billion-dollar company to a trust dedicated to fighting climate change. This unconventional move, driven by empathy and shared values, secured the loyalty of employees and fostered a passionate community around the brand's environmental mission.

Furthermore, establishing diverse information channels – from friendly hallway chats to roller skate based channels – mirrors the importance of diversifying information sources in business. Relying solely on internal reports or executive opinions can create echo chambers, leading to disastrous decisions. Open communication, active listening, and cultivating trusted allies with varied perspectives provide a more holistic understanding of the market, competitors, and customer needs, equipping leaders with the necessary tools to navigate complex situations.

This resonates with the success of **Netflix**. By analyzing vast amounts of user data and conducting A/B testing, Netflix built a recommendation algorithm that accurately predicts viewer preferences, driving subscriber growth and content development decisions. Similarly, Warby Parker, the online eyewear retailer, used social media and customer feedback to identify unmet needs and design trendy, affordable glasses, disrupting the traditional industry.

While information can be a powerful tool, it demands responsible utilization. The unethical manipulation of data or the use of insider information for personal gain can tarnish reputations and erode trust. Leaders must balance the need for intelligence with ethical considerations and ensure information is used for the greater good, not personal gain or manipulation.

Leadership demands more than just decisiveness and action. It requires a strategic mind, an empathetic heart, and the ability to harness the power of information. By cultivating diverse intelligence networks, understanding the motivations of stakeholders, and using information responsibly, leaders can navigate the complex chessboard of the business world, build sustainable success, and forge a future where collaboration and shared understanding drive progress.

Remember, Scar's downfall wasn't just his brute force approach; it was his blind reliance on poor information and a failure to understand the needs of his people. Understanding the needs and motivations of allies is equally crucial and the Gwai story also highlights the importance of nuance and human connection. Even as a blundering juvenile, I recognized that Gwai's neutrality stemmed not from fear, but from their contentment, and I adapted my approach accordingly. This understanding of different perspectives and motivations is crucial for any leader seeking to build alliances and navigate complex social dynamics. Tashinga's initial reluctance to join the fight highlights the importance of addressing concerns and demonstrating shared values. The recognition of their neutrality due to Scar's neglect offers a valuable lesson in understanding the perspectives of potential allies and crafting strategies that resonate with them.

This empathy-driven approach resonates with historical leaders like Nelson Mandela, who prioritized reconciliation and understanding over retribution after years of apartheid. By recognizing the shared humanity between himself and his former oppressors, he built a nation on the foundation of mutual respect and understanding, a stark contrast to the divisive tactics often employed by leaders who rely solely on brute force and misinformation.

Our spy network also echoed the power of espionage throughout history. The British "Enigma" code-breaking operation during World War II, led by Alan Turing and others, provided crucial insights into German military strategy, contributing significantly to Allied victory. In the Cold War, both sides engaged in elaborate espionage networks, gathering vital intel through covert operations and human intelligence sources.

While espionage can be ethically dubious, its undeniable influence on the course of history reinforces the importance of responsible information gathering and utilization. Leaders must utilize such means cautiously, balancing the need for intelligence with ethical considerations and making sure the information is employed for the greater good, not personal gain or manipulation.

Leadership demands more than just bravery and strength. It requires a strategic mind, an empathetic heart, and the ability to harness the power of information. By cultivating diverse intelligence networks, understanding the motivations of allies and adversaries alike, and using information not for manipulation but for progress, leaders can navigate the complex chessboard of conflict and build a future where collaboration trumps domination, and progress thrives on shared understanding.

As we face the challenges of our own time, remember that true victory lies not in conquering opponents, but in building bridges of understanding and forging a path towards a better future, together.

Adaptation

I sent a message to Josh to come and see me at Odzi. As the skaters went off, I stood with Tadiwa, watching as the civilian kids went off to train with Number 2 as their teacher. According to him, they weren't as unskilled as we assumed and training them was more than worthwhile. I didn't mind, the more fighters the better.

Josh finally arrived. His assignment had been to seek out discarded broom sticks and bring them to Odzi; the mission was a success. He dropped the sticks on the ground and stood over them proudly. Whilst Ngezi and Manyame employed their metal bars, broom sticks would give us more range and might give us an edge that would allow us to overcome their skill.

"Take one" I said as Tadiwa and I each calmly picked up a broom stick ourselves.

Josh had weapons training. Not a lot because he wasn't advanced enough in his martial arts studies. Being the naughty kid he was, he had started teaching himself to wield the Bo staff though. Josh nodded in response to my request and used his foot to flick a stick up and into his hands, twirled it around effortlessly and then stood in a fairly intimidating stance. I had never been able to tell if Josh was actually trained in kung fu or only half legit like me, but in this moment none of that really mattered. His skill was evident. I looked at him, then smiled.

"Good, now teach us."

7

When A Plan Comes together

We had a week to plan and apply our Bo staff training. We were running out of holiday time so we had to move quickly. Thanks to our network, we knew that all we had to do was defeat Manyame, and Ngezi might fall into place. This was no small task though. This same Manyame had somehow subdued the fearsome Ngezi, so a fight there was going to be highly difficult, but better that than fighting both courts one after the other. Unfortunately there was no way we were going to advance quickly enough in staff training to actually fight Manyame, not when they had been sword training for ages. No matter how much I wanted this to play out like an action movie training montage, this would simply not work out. We needed another tactic. I needed a private meeting with Nyasha.

As I mentioned earlier, Nyasha, the Manyame leader, and I

had "dated" as kids. We were so close that our parents became friends and they were still friends even though Nyasha and I hadn't really talked in a long time. This relationship between our parents made it quite easy to convince my mother to pay Nyasha's mother a visit and take me with her.

The sun was setting when my mother and I walked to Manyame. This was perfect because I needed to stay hidden. We walked briskly and got to Nyasha's place on the far side of Manyame whilst the sun was still visible on the horizon. My mother rang the door bell and waited. Nyasha opened the door.

The spies had completely undersold her muscular physique. She was slightly shorter than me but built like a little brick. She looked like she could rip me in two with little effort. Nyasha stared at me for a moment, scowling, then smiled as she turned to my mother. He voice was still as high as I remembered,

"Hi mama, come in, long time!" she squeaked.

My mom walked in. As I began to follow, Nyasha's arm blocked me from entering the house. Her voice grew deeper, more menacing,

"Why?"

"We need to talk" I said, matching her menace.

She moved her arm and let me in. We performed all the normal pleasantries, greeted each other's parents etc, then Nyasha invited me to her room to catch up. The parents nodded, barely paying attention to us at this point and eager to share stories and vent or whatever adults talked about. Nyasha led me to her room, shut the door behind us and then sat on her bed.

"What?"

I paused for a moment and looked around.

"You changed stuff. What happened to your dolls?"

Nyasha, still scowling, sighed and chose to humor me.

"I'm 10, Aaron, I don't play with dolls anymore."

"Yeah" I muttered, "just swords…"

Nyasha's scowl softened. She stood up and got right in my face.

"Yes, I play with swords, while you fight for girls like an idiot"

This was getting out of hand. 10 year old roast battles could easily devolve into violence because neither of us had the emotional fortitude to get insulted (even this lightly) without losing it or crying.

"Look, Scar is a problem. He took Zambezi and soon he will come for all of us."

"You took Bhubhi, so whats the difference?" she retorted.

In earnest, there wasn't a difference, not from her perspective.

Granted Scar would be brutal about his takeover, but ultimately Nyasha was going to fight for her people's independence regardless. Our shared history had gotten me into the room, but my campaign had stalled everything.

"Fine, how about you set the terms for battle."

Nyasha stepped back. She seemed to be deep in thought. What strategic advantage could I possibly gain from allowing her to set terms. The offer was too tempting though.

"Okay, so we go tomorrow. A one on one fight. First, we show each other our skills, then we battle.

"Can we make it two on two?" I asked.

"Sure, fine. Two on two. But you have to fight and that guy Josh can't fight."

I feigned deep thought for a moment, then agreed.

"Okay, what time, Queen Nyasha?"

"12."

I nodded again, struggling not to smile. This was perfect. The plan was working out as intended. Now on to the next step.

For the next hour, Nyasha and I caught up on life since Kindergarten. It was very awkward at first, but soon our old friendship's embers began to glow. She told me about how being bullied had forced her to become stronger. Her older cousin, a body builder, had started teaching her how to work out and she was loving the progress. More often than not, her figure was enough to dissuade any further bullying and the persistent ones were taken care off in fights.

I detailed my account of how the battle had begun. I told her about training my people to fight their own bullies and how that grew into the powerful dedication to martial arts that we all developed. I confided in her how my feelings for Rumbi had led me to make errors in judgment and how Scar, also acting on his feelings for Rumbi, had attacked my people and sparked this war. I told her all about how Josh, Tadiwa, Number 2, Paida, Dereck and Simba were my brothers and how we were expanding the family by taking over courts.

She in turn told me about her gang, Tanaka, Leo, Hussein and Josh aka Jojo (I convinced her that her Josh should be named Jojo to avoid confusion) and how much she loved those boys and how Leo had always served as her incredibly capable second in command. We laughed, we sympathized, we raged.

Basically, we bonded and rekindled our friendship.

At the height of all this invigorating conversation, my mother came to Nyasha's room and informed me it was time to leave. Nyasha and I looked at each other and our smiles slowly faded. Tomorrow, our courts would fight. Our friendship had rekindled, but that changed nothing about our responsibilities to our people.

At 12, the next day, we would be opponents in a battle that would determine the course of this war.

***

The next day, noon came.

I had picked Tadiwa, my trusted second in command with whom I had defeated Brian and claimed Bhubhi, to be my fighting partner once more. We walked to Manyame, bo staves in hand. Nyasha, her whole gang and Ngezi's gang waited patiently. They looked formidable, swords in hand, ready for battle. I imagine we looked intimidating too. Showing up with no back up was a purposeful move meant to convey our complete confidence in our skills. Seeing this massive collection of bad asses made me regret that decision a little, but we had a plan, the plan would work. It had to.

Finally, we were face to face. Nyasha and her overwhelming force, Tadiwa and I with our sticks. There was no sign of friendliness on Nyasha's face as she began the proceedings.

"Lets do this. First, we show you what we can do."

What followed was an impressive display of sword skills. From an onlookers perspective it probably looked like a bunch of kids clumsily waving about metal bars and randomly poking at the air, but to us gathered there, we were witnessing a perfectly coordinated and intimidating death dance.

Finally it was our turn.

Now is a good time to go back to an earlier conversation Tadiwa, Josh and I had. Remember in the conclusion of the previous chapter, when I told Josh to "teach us". As much as it was really dramatic to end the conversation there, it went far beyond that. Josh had asked what he should teach us and I had replied,

"teach us to look like we can fight with sticks."

The main point being "LOOK LIKE". There was no way we could learn to fight well with sticks and we knew Manyame would never put their swords away willingly, so we had to intimidate them into it. Our spies had told us that Nyasha had taken Ngezi by first insisting on seeing a display of their skill then pushing the battle toward their weaknesses. Basic logic told us that if we looked good enough with weapons, she would 100% opt not to use weapons.

Next, we had to get Nyasha to make the decision to have an exhibition again, just in case she had it in her head to change tactics, hence the visit, the roasting and the allowing her to set terms.

Now, back to the display.

Tadiwa and I had rehearsed a fight for the past week and that served as our display. We went at each other ferociously, it looked like we were trying to murder each other, but in truth this was more a display of trust than it was an attempt to harm. We knew the moves and we trusted each other to strike true as much as we trusted each other to block perfectly.

By the time the display ended, the looks on the Ngezi forces where those of total shock. They had just witnessed friends trying to kill each other. Even they held back with their swords and always made an effort not to maim.

Nyasha betrayed no fear, but I knew her well enough to see the hesitation in her eyes.

"Cool," she said authoritatively, " Now the terms for the fight… No weapons."

BINGO.

It took all our self restraint to stop us celebrating. Instead, we nodded and threw our sticks to the ground. Nyasha stepped forward and Leo, a tall lanky kid, stepped forward as well. The rest of their gang stepped back and formed a circle. The two on two fight had begun.

Nyasha rushed me as Leo engaged Tadiwa. I'm not too sure of the details of Tadiwa's fight because I had Nyasha to contend with, and contend we did. Nyasha was as strong as I was, but slightly slower. I landed blow after blow, but she just kept coming. Eventually she wrestled me to the ground and got me in a flawed choke hold. I escaped and reversed it. She managed to throw me off her back and we were back at it on our feet.

This cycle went on for quite some time. A glance at Tadiwa told me his fight was going pretty much similarly. About 15 minutes later, we were all barely moving. We were out of breath and couldn't, for the life of us muster up the strength to throw another blow.

Now the second part of the visit needed to come in clutch.

Nyasha and I may have been locked in battle, but we were friends.

"Ny…Nyasha…" I muttered.

"What?"

"We are evenly matched" I said as I sat down.

Nyasha, Tadiwa and Leo followed suite, thoroughly exhausted.

"No one is going to win."

Nyasha rested her head on her arms and her arms on her knees. She waited a moment and then she finally caught her breath.

"We can get other fighters?"

I shook my head and motioned toward Leo and Tadiwa, "Then what? More people get hurt?"

Nyasha turned her head and saw how battered and bruised her friend was. She looked around and realized we were all bruised and battered. I was actually bleeding a little.

"Okay, so now what?" she asked, deflated.

"How about, you keep your courts, but whenever you need help, Odzi will always come to help, and whenever we need help, like say in a battle with Scar, you swear to show up and fight."

Nyasha considered this proposal for a moment. She stood up and we all followed suite. She glanced at our sticks, then looked me in the eye.

"I know I will keep my word…," She said, trailing off.

I nodded and replied, "And you know I will keep mine too."

"Fine," she finally said as she picked up my stick and handed it to me. Before she could pick up her sword, I used my foot to flick it up into my hand, just like Josh had taught me, and then handed it to her.
   "Partners."

Nyasha nodded, "partners."

Don't you just love it when a plan comes together?

War

Two days later, the sun rose on the day of war. This was it. The last battle. The day I would either lose everything or free everyone. Chances were, though, we were about to be defeated spectacularly.

Let's rewind to the day after Nyasha and I reached an agreement, which also happened to be the day preceding the final battle. An eerie silence had fallen upon all of Eastview. Hardly any kids were outside playing, there was no training anywhere and there were no roller skates or bikes moving about. Even I was seated alone in the house, watching cartoon reruns. I had scheduled the final battle of this wretched war for the next day and encouraged everyone to take it easy. The spy network being quiet meant we didn't know what Mupfure was up to, but at this point it didn't matter. We had overwhelming force and skilled fighters on our side. Ngezi alone could give Mupfure a hard time, let alone a unified force of Ngezi, Manyame, Odzi and our giant from Bhubhi.

All of this should have given me confidence, but in truth I was nervous. Scar was the real deal, a true threat. Ngezi and Manyame had been softened by Nyasha's friendly affection, but Scar had no mercy. He was a mad man, incapable of negotiation or empathy. He was the bogey man!

Suddenly someone rang the door bell. My mom had taught me never to open the door unless I knew and trusted the person on the other side, so I asked who was there.

"Scar."

Oh no. Was this an ambush? Had my order to have everyone gather strength for tomorrow a grave miscalculation?

"Don't worry, I'm alone."

I didn't believe him. This brute was incapable of honesty. How the hell did he find out where I live? Were there spies watching us? Was Scar…smart?!

The front of the house was visible from a high window in the kitchen, so I climbed up and looked outside. Scar was standing in the corridor, alone. I looked around and saw no one else around. I climbed down, took a moment to gather myself and then unlocked and opened the door. Scar smiled as he laid eyes on me. I had never really officially met him. All our fights and issues had been from a distance, so finally seeing him now felt strange. He was a lot shorter than I assumed. His face did indeed have some scars, but not a lot. He looked almost perfectly normal and at face value he might have been, had it not been for the cruelty he had wrought over Eastview.

"Whats up man?" he said cheerfully.

"What do you want?"

He frowned, feigning insult.

"May I come in?"he said poking his head into the house.

"Ha! No."

"Fair. I came over because I wanted to give you a chance to surrender."

I laughed. It wasn't even on purpose or an act of mockery. I was genuinely shocked by how stupid this proposition was. Scar simply smiled and shrugged. His demeanor betrayed no fear or dread.

"I know you have united the courts. I know you have a solid army. I know you are coming for us tomorrow. I also know you are going to lose."

I stopped laughing. Something about his tone was getting to me. Scar wasn't scared and I was almost totally sure he wasn't bluffing. He knew something I didn't. He had some sort of secret weapon or re-enforcements.

"You don't have a chance against us Scar," I said with a forced smile on my face, "maybe you should surrender."

Scar shook his head in disappointment.

"Look kid, if you surrender now, I take Odzi and leave your stupid little alliance alone. But if we battle tomorrow, I take everything."

And there it was. Scar had not attacked us once as we gathered our allies. He had allowed us to move freely, recruit who we wanted, fight all these battles, lay out strategies, networks and communication lines without once retaliating. We had gathered weapons, numbers, grounds and knowledge and now we were a plumb cow ready for slaughter. How had I missed this?! I had played perfectly into his plan. I underestimated his intelligence whilst dancing to his tune the entire time. If I surrender now, he takes my court. If we lose tomorrow, he takes EVERYONE.

We had not created a united army to battle Mupfure.

We had created Scar's Kingdom for him.

I stood there frozen. I had been completely outmaneuvered. All these efforts to become a great leader had betrayed me. I couldn't hide the devastation. My mouth dropped open and tears welled up in my eyes. Scar giggled.

"So, what will it be?"

No. My time as leader had to have been worth something.

"See you tomorrow, Scar."

I didn't let him reply. I slammed the door shut and sank to the floor, tears flowing down my face. How could this have happened? I could hear Scar's laughter fading as he walked back to his court. He was so assured of victory. I had to act.

I checked the kitchen window again and found no one in sight. I then rushed over to Tadiwa's house. I rang the door bell and Tadiwa opened the door. Upon seeing my best friend, I broke down in tears. Tadiwa was confused, but immediately invited me in. I gathered myself and started shaking my head.

"We made his kingdom for him."

"What?"

"Scar…he came to my house. He told me he knows about everything and we are still going to lose and if he wins he takes everything!"

Tadiwa's eyes started to well up too.

"No…no way."

I nodded, "yeah man. He played us."

Paida walked into the room and was shocked to find his two older brothers in tears. The sight alone was enough to fill his eyes with tears before we even explained.

"What's going on?" he asked, his voice shuddering.

I explained it all to him as I dried my tears. He started to cry too. We went to Number 2's house, a shuddering mess of tears and snot, full of fear and confusion and rang his door bell. Number 2 opened the door and stared at us. We explained the full situation to him, but he didn't cry. In fact he seemed entirely unmoved.

"So?"

We stared back at him, mystified.

"What do you mean 'so'? So we might lose everything!" I screamed.

"All due respect boss, shut up."

His words caught me by surprise. I had been hunched over in defeat, but now I stood up straight.

"What did you say?"

Number 2 sighed. "Aaron, what did you have before all this happened?"

I paused for a moment. "Nothing?"

"Wow, you can't be this clueless. How are you even leading us, man?"

Number 2 was starting to cross a line, so I stepped forward to let him know to get to the point and fast. He raised his hands to signify that he had no intention of fighting and then pointed at Tadiwa and Paida.

"Oh," I said as I finally realized what he meant.

"Aaron, in the past year, you have grown into someone I truly respect. I remember the first day I realized you might be special. Remember the day you let Paida win at wrestling?"

Paida gasped.

"Sorry man, its true," I mumbled.

Paida shrugged and giggled. He knew. Of course he knew.

"I understand that this whole war thing has a lot resting on it, but win our lose, you will still be a great leader and you will still have us, your family. And no matter what happens, we will give Scar hell."

I had no words. I gathered the three of them into my arms and held them for a while. The embrace was exactly what the doctor ordered. I wasn't the same kid who had stood by as Jacob hurt my family, I was a mighty leader now and I sure as hell wasn't alone. No matter what Scar brought the next day, we would face it as a family.

***

Back to the day of battle.

I betrayed no fear as I watched our forces gather. Brian and Josh showed up with Bhubhi in tow, Nyasha came through on her promise and brought both Ngezi and Manyame armed and ready; even little Tashinga showed up to represent Gwai. Many of the civilians from all the courts showed up too. There were at least 60-80 of us. Normally, the leader of such a mighty force gives a speech to get his troops pumped, but there was no speech to be given. I simply stood in front of the massive army and breathed.

Tadiwa came to my side and put his hand on my shoulder. I looked at him and nodded.

I looked at the army and completely misquoted Brave Heart.

"LETS DO THIS FOR OUR FREEDOM!"

The army yelled back and we, as a unit, jogged to Mupfure. It wasn't a long distance but I like to imagine the march in slow motion. Swords, bikes, roller skates, bo staves and even a giant among us. We must have looked fantastic (In reality it was obviously a small mob of uncoordinated kids, but stay with me).

I'm not too sure what I expected to see when we got to Mupfure, but a small group of about 10 or so kids wasn't it. Yet, there they were, Scar and about 9 other kids standing in our way. I was wary of traps so I stopped the army in its tracks. It took a few yells from the other leaders to get everyone to be quiet, but eventually there was complete silence. Scar regarded our army calmly with a huge grin on his face.

I took a deep breath. We were about to learn what Scars great plan was and possibly lose this battle. I already had a rebellion plotted in my mind should Scar become King. I was ready for defeat. Scar stepped forward, drew a deep breath and yelled,

"We choose beyblade."

For a full 30 seconds, nobody moved or made a sound. You could practically see the confusion weaving between our young minds. I had all but forgotten about the rules of war I had set out prior to confronting Bhubhi. Either beyblade, a fight or both. The rules had technically only been evoked once, but regardless, this was still absolutely within Scar and Mupfure's rights.

"One match. One round. A battle royale. Three of your best versus three of our best."

Still, no one said anything. Scar had surely lost his mind. We understood that he had no choice but to move away from an actual fight. Our assumption was Zambezi had heard about this battle and opted out, along with a majority of his forces, leaving him with a few faithful soldiers. But beyblade? We had the greatest beybladers from both Bhubhi and Odzi gathered on our side. What the hell was this?

"Tadiwa, Number 2, you're with me" I yelled.

From Scar's side, two kids stepped forward. One whose name I don't recall, but recognized as Scar's lieutenant and the other, the new rich kid we had spied moving in a while ago. We will call them Mystery and New Kid respectively. We made our way back to Odzi where the best and widest corridors could be found and stuffed ourselves into the area around the elevators where the corridor was widest. I glanced over at Nyasha. She seemed thoroughly annoyed that she wouldn't get to beat someone up today, but she seemed just as curious as everyone else about what was about to happen. The fate of her court and many others rested, not on our strength, but on a game! Considering we were just kids playing at war commanders, this felt somewhat poetic.

Tadiwa, Number 2 and I took our beyblades out of our pockets and wrapped them in their draw strings. We glanced between each other, looking for answers to what Scar was up to but found nothing among ourselves. The corridor was dark now thanks to all the kids blocking most of the sunlight, but there was just enough light for us to see something strange glisten in New Kid's hand as Scar's team prepared their beyblades. They stepped forward in unison and that's when we saw it. There was an audible gasp throughout the crowd as New Kid revealed his beyblade.

Scar and Mystery's beyblades were standard spray can tops just like ours, but New Kid's family was wealthy; their kid couldn't be seen playing with makeshift nonsense, no, New Kid had a **real beyblade.**

It was made of plastic and metal, manufactured with design specs based on the actual show. It had sharp, dangerous looking edges, arranged into layers of menacing spirals. This was the real deal. We did not have a chance. This was Scar's secret weapon, and it got worse. Scar noticed us staring at New Kid's beyblade and felt the need to add to our shock.

"Its got reverse spin too, do you even know what that is?"

We said nothing, so he continued, "Reverse spin means it will spin in one direction until it stops, then it will automatically get up and start spinning again in the other direction. It does double the time!"

The crowd began to murmur. Hope was declining fast and fear was setting in.

Suddenly, Josh yelled for everyone to shut up. He looked at me and nodded, a look of determination on his face. For a kid whose future rested on spinning spray can tops beating a perfectly manufactured bad ass toy, Josh was oddly confident.

I looked at the faces of my people, at their eyes. Some filled with fear, others with brutish determination and others still with the passivity of one who had seen many a battle. I looked at the leaders, Josh, Brian, Nyasha and Hussein. Each powerful and capable in their own regard, looking to me for any sign of hope, trusting me with their people. If we were going to lose today, I was going to make sure my people went down with a mighty leader at the helm.

I gritted my teeth and prepared to launch.

Brian stepped up to referee.

"3, 2, 1, LET 'EM RIP!"

I launched my beyblade with everything I had. Fueled by my people's hope, determination and trust. I put every once of training, blood, sweat and tears I had put into this campaign into that rip and spun the beyblade faster than I ever had before or ever did since.

The arena was chaos. All 6 of the beyblades began crashing into each other. The dark environment allowed us to see occasional sparks, which prompted cheers and gasps from our spectators. It felt like we were actually in the anime. Mystery and Number 2's beyblades crashed violently into each other and both stopped, prompting gasps from the audience. They retrieved their tops and withdrew into the crowd. Next, Tadiwa's beyblade was sent flying by New Kids monstrosity. Even I gasped at that. The amount of power I was facing was insane. The clash had slowed New Kid down, but he was still a threat. Scar's simply stopped spinning on its own, his launch had been that of an untrained beyblader so this outcome was expected.

It was down to me and the New Kid. I could see mine beginning to slow down. I was getting worried. New Kid's beyblade wobbled a few times, then stopped. Everyone waited with baited breath. It lurched, then slowly began to spin again in the opposite direction, just as Scar had said. I didn't know what to do. What chance did I have?

"Come on buddy!" I yelled, "You can do it!"

That's right, I was calling upon my bit beast. I knew it was nonsense. I knew there was no point, but I had nowhere else to turn.

"PLEASE!"

It was Tadiwa who began the chant.

"YOU. CAN. DO. IT."

Soon, everyone was chanting. Hell, I was chanting!

Scar found it all ridiculous, he laughed maliciously as we chanted out souls out. At least, he did until New Kid's Beyblade wobbled toward danger. There were little water gutters (I think that's what they were), no more than 2 centimeters deep and 1 centimeter wide on the edges of the corridors. They were a beyblades nightmare and New Kid's beyblade was heading right for one. The crowd grew quiet.

We watched, in complete silence as my beyblade slowly inched toward New Kid's. Both were moving incredibly slow at this point. Finally, my beyblade gently tapped New Kid's, sending the highly advanced toy into the gutter and stopping it immediately. My Beyblade spun for 3 or 4 more revolutions, then did something relatively unheard of – it stopped while remaining perfectly upright.

The crowd's roar was deafening.

I walked over to my toy, picked it up and leaped into the embrace of my people. We had won! The battle was over!

"YOU!" I yelled with my finger pointed at Scar's forehead.

"You will never bully or hurt anyone again. Your gang is done! Your rule is done! If you ever try anything on anyone again, even in your own damn court, I will come for you and I will bring my entire kingdom with me to crush you! Do you understand?"

I wasn't sure what movie character I had just channeled, in fact, I wasn't channeling anyone. This was me, and I liked it. Scar, not as much. The hatred in his eyes gave way to defeat. He looked at the united force standing before him and sighed.

"Yes, I understand".

We yelled at the top of our lungs. Victory was ours!

Thus, there was peace in the Kingdom of Eastview, united under a King forged in the fires of adversity and conquest, then quenched in the waters of empathy and selflessness.

Learning, initially, that standing by as injustice is perpetrated enables the ruthless, I had grown slowly. Entering for a time into the darkness of deception, and then, in those depths, learning the value of humility, I emerged ultimately as a strategic and compassionate leader who united five independent courts to overthrow a looming menace. A tale of brotherly love, romance, and determination, concluded with a celebration of the childishness of all who participated, combined with a celebration of freedom that echoed throughout Eastview.

Through the exploits of a child we have grown to understand leadership through lessons about the value of resilience in failure, the power of community and collaboration, the double edge sword of valor, the vitality of information, the value of a strategic mind, the power of diplomacy and most importantly, the importance of making sure to lead for the sake of those you lead, and never from a place of selfish ambition.

In the end, I was only King for a day. I had not sought this position to rule, after all; I had risen to power to attain freedom. Now, with the goal fulfilled, all courts were granted their independence, and all leaders returned to governing their own people. Of course if a threat had risen again our unification, powered by our new found bonds, would have been far easier; however no new threat ever came. Eastview was truly free.

In this moment though, I was still the king of Eastview Gardens. I had the power to unify all of us for at least one activity on this, our independence day. After the noise died down and Scar had slunk back to Mupfure, I looked at my people and declared in my most regal voice,

"LETS PLAY OPEN GATES."

About the Author

Takunda Aaron Chimutashu aka Zen ISA is an award-winning Film Director, Writer, Photographer and Pan African with a background in Engineering, Entrepreneurship and Social leadership. He is the founder and Creative Director of Immortal African Studios and co-founder and resident Film Director of award-winning production house, Visual Sensations Media. As a self-titled "Universal Creative" Zen loves to explore art in all its forms and seeks to investigate all the amazing ways art can influence and inspire our society for the better.

Having acquired an Honors Degree in Mechatronic Engineering at University and explored his passion for social leadership through volunteering at Harare City Junior Council for nearly a decade (Initially as the Junior Mayor of Harare ad subsequently as a Respectable Junior Alderman), Zen found himself still hungry to learn and expand. It was through this hunger and the subsequent journey to sate it that he found himself on film sets doing technical jobs like being set engineer or a grip. Witnessing films and TV shows being made created a deep and powerful passion for Filmmaking in him and set off his journey to becoming a full time filmmaker. Now, Zen is a Film Director,

Producer, Author, Writer, Documentarian and Photographer who has made it his mission to document and grow African stories through the visual medium.

At the core of Zen's growth are the principles of Pan-Africanism. All this combined means Zen's greatest desire is to create books and films that facilitate the growth of a vibrant and diverse community of African leaders across all industries who can use their skills and abilities to unite their people in an effort to empower African communities and contribute to the continent's overall development. .